THE CELTIC MYSTIQUE

The foundation of the Celtic Mystique comprises such names as Cousy, Sharman, and Macauley. The pivotal figure of that early era, without question, was Bill Russell. The next era was anchored by John Havlicek. Now we are living in what everyone in Boston refers to as the Larry Bird era. The unifying thread that binds this 30-year tradition is Arnold "Red" Auerbach.

The vehicles that help convey the tradition are Boston Garden's parquet floor and the banners. It's a terrible playing floor, unquestionably the worst in the league. It's got notorious dead spots and chunks gouged out of it. But when the floor has just been polished, and the TV cameras catch it from above, it's the most impressive playing surface in the world. To millions of people, that floor *means* professional basketball."

— from *Cousy on The Celtic Mystique*

COUSY

ON THE CELTIC MYSTIQUE

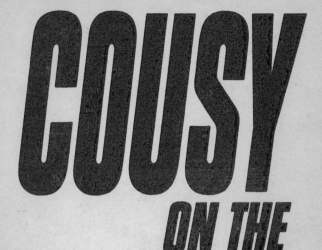

BOB COUSY AND BOB RYAN

ZEBRA BOOKS
KENSINGTON PUBLISHING CORP.

ZEBRA BOOKS

are published by

Kensington Publishing Corp.
475 Park Avenue South
New York, NY 10016

First Zebra Books printing: March, 1990

Printed in the United States of America

To our new treasures who
have so enriched our lives—
Nicole, Marie,
and Zachery Park

B.C.

Table of Contents

Prologue

THE LOS ANGELES Lakers are the champions of the basketball world in 1988. They have won five NBA championships in the decade, and their coach, Pat Riley, wants very much for his team to be known as "The Team of the Eighties."

Very well. The Lakers are the Team of the Eighties. But when it comes to identifying the NBA franchise that has a right to the claim of "America's Team," there is only one selection—the Boston Celtics. No basketball team in the world stirs up passions the way the Boston Celtics do.

The Celtics haven't won a title since 1986, but to the basketball fans of America they stand for something very special. What they have that L.A. doesn't have yet is over thirty years of tradition. The Celtics will always have that tradition, at least as long as Red Auerbach is around.

Los Angeles has a great basketball team, no question. But ask yourself: what is the first thing you think about when you think of the Lakers? Kareem Abdul-

Jabbar's Sky Hook? Magic Johnson's lookaway passes?
James Worthy's fast break dunks? That's what you *should*
think about. But if you're the average American basketball fan, you think about the Laker Girls, Jack
Nicholson, or Dyan Cannon jumping up at the sight of
the CBS camera. You think of the entire "showtime"
image coveted by Laker owner Dr. Jerry Buss. Is this
unfair to Riley and his athletes? Of course it is.

What about Boston, which trails the Lakers, five
championships to three, in the Eighties? What's the first
thing the average American basketball fan thinks about
when imagining the Celtics? There are two things, actually, and they go hand in hand. Fans think about the
parquet floor and the banners hanging proudly from
the Boston Garden rafters. There is a big difference in
what they're *selling* in Los Angeles and what they're
selling in Boston. That's why there is a verifiable Celtic
Mystique. There is no Laker Mystique, as great a team
as the Lakers have been.

Walter Brown founded the Celtics in 1946, but during
the first four years of the team's existence there was
nothing to distinguish the franchise. The team made
the playoffs only once (1948) and was promptly elim-
inated by Chicago in two games. Brown needed a coach
following the 1949–50 season. A hockey man by inclination, Brown loved his Celtics as an institution, but
everything he knew about the technicalities of basketball could be recorded on a matchbook cover. He followed the advice of such advisors as Sam Cohen, the
sports editor of the *Boston Record*, and hired thirty-two
year old Arnold "Red" Auerbach, who had coached both
the Washington Capitols and Tri-Cities Hawks. This
remarkable odd couple relationship was to last until
the death of Walter Brown in 1964.

Auerbach tried to shape the Celtics immediately. One
of his first pronouncements was that he wanted abso-

lutely no part of yours truly. I was something of a local favorite, having played four years of college basketball at Holy Cross. The school is located in Worcester, only thirty-five miles from downtown Boston.

Red went so far as to inquire of his new owner during a luncheon one day whether he was supposed to be constructing a ball club using his best judgment, or satisfying "the local yokels" who were hoping the Celtics would draft me. This was not the foundation for a lasting partnership under ordinary circumstances, but it certainly was quintessential Red Auerbach. And if it is possible for me to be objective, I would have resisted taking me, too. In basketball you start building a team with big frontline people, not with skinny 6′ guards.

Auerbach eventually did wind up with me, and we spent thirteen years together. We helped construct the beginning of the Celtic Mystique. Red is still there, thirty-eight years later, trying to put together another championship team. I'm still there too, as a broadcaster.

The foundation of the Celtic Mystique comprises names such as Cousy, Sharman, and Macauley. The pivotal figure of that early era, without question, was Bill Russell. The next era was anchored by John Havlicek and featured the likes of Dave Cowens, Jo Jo White, Don Nelson, and Paul Silas. Now we are living in what everyone in Boston refers to as the Larry Bird era, whose prime players include Kevin McHale, Robert Parish, Dennis Johnson, and Danny Ainge.

The unifying thread is Auerbach. The vehicles that help convey the tradition to new fans are the parquet floor and the flags. It's a terrible playing floor, unquestionably the worst in the league. It's got notorious dead spots and chunks gouged out of it. But when the floor has just been polished, and the TV cameras catch it from above, it is the most impressive playing surface in the world. To millions of people, that floor *means* professional basketball. Of course, it wouldn't mean much if the team playing on it went 29–53 every year. That's where Auerbach comes in.

Likewise, the championship banners are hard to ignore. There are sixteen championship flags, plus two banners carrying retired numbers, of which the Celtics have more than any team in professional sports. There used to be more banners up there. Back in the sixties, you would also find a banner for each division and conference championship. Then the Celtics started running out of space and began to limit themselves to championship flags only.

The Celtics have retired a lot of numbers, not to mention a name—Loscy. That would be Jungle Jim Loscutoff, whose number is also retired. He was one of the players wearing 18 before Dave Cowens wore it. To properly honor Loscutoff when retiring his number, his nickname itself was also written out on the banner.

The retired numbers are 6 (Bill Russell), 10 (Jo Jo White), 14 (me), 15 (Tom Heinsohn), 16 (Satch Sanders), 17 (John Havlicek), 18 (Cowens and Loscutoff), 19 (Don Nelson), 21 (Bill Sharman), 22 (Ed Macauley), 23 (Frank Ramsey), 24 (Sam Jones), and 25 (K.C. Jones). In addition, there is a symbolic 1 for Walter Brown and a symbolic 2 for Auerbach himself.

That's a lot of numbers, and in the minds of some people there have been a lot of borderline decisions in retiring them. Given the pattern already established, several more numbers will go up during the next few years, starting with Bird's 33. McHale (32), Parish (00), Dennis Johnson (3), and Ainge (44) are other possibilities. Sometimes people joke that the Celtics aren't far away from using the first number like 34A.

The proliferation of retired numbers speaks to the very heart of Celtic Mystique. The Celtics aren't as selective as other organizations when it comes to honoring their players, at least not in terms of tangible accomplishments. By retiring the numbers of players such as Loscutoff, Sanders, and Nelson, who never got close to an All-Star Game, the Celtics have proclaimed to the world that their concept of what is and what isn't important differs from everyone else's. Auerbach has never put this down on paper. He has never said, "By honoring a Don Nelson, I am trying to impress fans in New Orleans or Keokuk that by choosing to root for the Celtics they have chosen an elite organization." That wouldn't occur to Red. But that is exactly what has happened. And if any other organization tries to emulate the Celtics in this manner now, however respectfully, it will come off as little more than a copycat maneuver.

— 1 —

Arnold "Red" Auerbach

FEELINGS ABOUT THE Celtics run deep in the NBA, and not even the passage of time—in some cases, *lots* of time—can dim the passion of those who have fought against them over the years.

Take something as innocuous as the Legends Game now played each year as part of the NBA All-Star Weekend. You'd think that when a bunch of guys in their forties and fifties (we won't include the feelings of the guys in their thirties, many of whom wish they were still playing in the league) get together for a fun game, there would be a limit to the competitiveness. There isn't.

I coached the East team in the 1988 game at Chicago Stadium. It just so happens we won the game in sudden death overtime when Dave Cowens scored on an offensive rebound. Okay, so he practically shoved a defender into the fifth row to get the rebound. It's just a fun afternoon, right? The game is meaningless, right?

That's what I thought. But I found that every player brings his own baggage to these events. I've always had a very close relationship with Dolph Schayes. He's a nice, gentle man. But I'll never forget him coming up to me after the game and saying, "Nothing ever changes in this goddamned league. The Celtics are going to find a way to cheat or do something to win." The hatred is deep.

I spent time during a trip to New York last year with Al Bianchi, general manager of the Knicks. He broke into the NBA in the fifties, and had a decade-long playing career with the Syracuse Nationals and then the Philadelphia 76ers. I realize a lot of people in the league resent the Celtics for their success, but Al carries it to an extreme.

Bianchi wears a ring. At first glance it looks like a green onyx ring, but when you look at it closer you see that it has an inscription that says, "Phoenix Suns, 1976 World Champions," or words to that effect. Inside the ring is another inscription, and this one you wouldn't believe if you hadn't seen it. It says, "Fuck you, Richie Powers."

The story behind this is that Al Bianchi was the assistant coach of the Suns in 1976. The Suns had gone 42–40 in the regular season, but they got rolling in the playoffs and advanced to the Finals, where their opponent happened to be the Celtics. Boston won Games One and Two in the Boston Garden and the Suns took the next two games in Phoenix. Game Five, played on Friday, June 4, turned out to be the epic triple overtime game, which Boston won by a 128–126 score.

What frosts Bianchi to this day is that at the end of regulation or at the end of the first overtime—I don't remember which—with the score tied, Boston gained possession of the basketball and Paul Silas asked for a timeout. But Boston was out of timeouts. The rule at the time was that a team asking for a timeout in excess of the allotted number would be granted one, but the opposing team would get to shoot a technical foul shot. Silas looked right at referee Richie Powers, pleading for the timeout. Powers looked right at Silas and waved his arms like a football official signaling an incomplete pass (as if to say, "Forget about it."). Had Powers called that timeout, the Suns could very well have won the game. Boston eventually won the championship, defeating the Suns in Game Seven.

When asked why he ignored Silas' obvious request for the timeout, Powers, an autocratic referee from the old school, said, "I didn't want the game to end that way." To Al Bianchi, the Celtics were being protected —once again. Hence the ring and the bizarre inscription.

What could produce such paranoia, such pure hatred? I think I can supply the answer in two words—Red Auerbach. The man has cast a big shadow over the NBA for 38 years. When people hear the name "Boston Celtics," the first thing they ordinarily think of is Red Auerbach and a puff of cigar smoke. If they're old enough, they conjure up the image of Red stomping the sidelines, screaming at officials, and waving the rolled-up scorecard that was one of his trademarks. They might think of him going nose-to-nose with a Sid Borgia. But most of all they think of Red lighting up a victory cigar when he was sure we'd win the game.

Red and the cigar. Paul Seymour, who played and coached in the NBA for many years, once told me that his ultimate ambition was not to win a league championship, but to crush the cigar in Red's face some night when the Celtics had slipped up and lost *after* Red had lit the cigar. Seymour never had the chance. Incidentally, at one point Seymour coached Bianchi. What do you suppose they talked about on train rides between road games?

*   *   *

You might acknowledge that Cousy, Sharman, and Macauley helped create interest in professional basketball in Boston, that Russell was the key ingredient that made the dynasty possible, and that Bird is the symbol of today's Celtics' success. But for the last thirty-eight years there is no doubt who the embodiment of the Celtics has been. When people think of the Celtics, they think of Red Auerbach. There is such a thing as the Celtic Mystique because since 1950 the team has been run by a driven man who has dedicated himself to victory. For almost four decades, the Celtics have reflected the spirit of Arnold J. "Red" Auerbach.

As a coach, Arnold wasn't fancy. He came from a different era. There were no extensive advance scouting reports and no videotapes to study. He believed in fast break basketball. He believed in spreading out the scoring load. He believed in bearing down on defense. He believed in conditioning. He was adamant that we get into good physical shape as quickly as possible so we could steal a few games early, get off to a good start and watch everybody try to catch us. Generally speaking, this is what happened every year, once we got Russell.

Arnold wasn't revolutionary. We had seven basic plays, plus options, year after year. He preached attention to detail. Set the pick properly. Run the play right. A foot —maybe even an inch—here or there could make a difference in the successful execution of a play. He believed in physical intimidation and does to this moment. He always found room for a muscle man who could set picks, plant an elbow in an opponent's kisser, and just plain keep order out there. Arnold was personally combative, and not above throwing a punch or two when things got rowdy, such as the time he and Hawks owner Ben Kerner—a former employer of his—exchanged punches prior to a playoff game in St. Louis.

For the six years we struggled without Russell, Arnold was basically a local phenomenon. We never got very far in the playoffs. In those days, there wasn't much national attention focused on our league, anyway. Ft. Wayne, Rochester, and Syracuse aren't exactly media centers. Arnold made his mark in Boston, but the Celtics were far behind the Red Sox and Bruins in local status.

Arnold was always cocky, but there is no question his personality expanded with success. The lighting of the cigar is as good an example as any. I doubt when he did it the first time that it was premeditated. Red smoked cigars, still does, and always will. There was no rule against it at the time. It all happened so quickly. If someone did a thing like that today, the league would undoubtedly take action. Look at what happened to Don Nelson when he wanted to wear basketball shoes with a logo while working the sidelines. He was forbidden to do so.

Red just went ahead and lit his cigar. Nobody said anything, and before long it caught on as a gimmick. It's about as arrogant an act as you can imagine in team sports. That symbolic act never burned him, either. He never got caught. I'm sure that after a while he began to give it a little more thought.

Red Auerbach has been both lucky and good. Most of the big gambles he's taken have panned out. Russell. Cowens. Bird. McHale. Parish. Ainge. In every case the guy was expected to be good, and he turned out to be even better. In the case of Russell and Bird, the dividends were unimaginable at the time the players joined the club. The same is true to a slightly lesser extent with Cowens. The Celtics have won sixteen championships, and those three players have been the cornerstones of all of them: eleven for Russell, two for Cowens, and three for Bird.

The only time the roll of the dice has really gone

against Arnold in a big way was in the case of Len Bias. When your luck goes bad, it generally goes bad for a while. The Celtics came up with a lot of injuries in 1986–87, but a lot of teams have had that problem. Surely, not having Bill Walton around has hurt the Celtics. He was a vital part of the 1985–86 championship team. I don't know how important Bias would have been that year. We went to the Finals, anyway. Would he have made a difference? Perhaps. But I can't guarantee a rookie would have changed the result. You don't know about rookies when the playoffs come. They're so erratic.

But Bias did reverse a trend. The big gambles and big trades have normally worked out for the Celtics. Absolutely. You need luck. Russell was a gamble in that we needed the cooperation of Ben Kerner, who owned St. Louis, and Lester Harrison, who owned Rochester, to get the rights to sign him. Bird came because the team had an extra first round draft pick, which means another team had screwed up. But I'll tell you this: whatever luck Auerbach has had he's known how to exploit it.

If there is a loophole, a rule that can be bent, a way to squeeze every drop of personal satisfaction from a situation, Arnold will find it. I should know.

In 1969, I had just become coach of the Cincinnati Royals. They were a team in transition. Early in the summer before the first season I decided that I might be able to help the team myself by playing when floor leadership and ballhandling might help win a game. I was forty years old. I wasn't going to scare anybody. However, rather than build for the future with our older superstars, Oscar Robertson and Jerry Lucas, it made more sense to go with a youth movement. So in the next year we traded both Oscar and Jerry and tried to draft some eager, aggressive young players.

There was only one problem: I still "belonged" to the Celtics. I was on the retired list, which made sense since I played my final game for Auerbach in 1963, six years earlier. In the meantime I had coached for six years at Boston College. It certainly never dawned on me that there would be any problem if I suited up for the Royals. If I wanted to go out and risk my reputation, why should Arnold care?

I should have known better. Auerbach wouldn't let me play for the Royals without "compensation." One minute I'm a name on a list and the next I'm an "asset." He wouldn't budge until we finally settled. The Royals had a player named Bill Dinwiddie. He was a 6'7" forward with some talent who would be sitting out the year with a knee injury. We transferred his contract to the Celtics. I wound up playing seven games before deciding maybe mine wasn't such a good idea after all. Dinwiddie played two years for the Celtics. For Arnold, it turned out to be a pretty good deal.

I still find this episode difficult to digest. My old coach. It seemed at the time such a cutthroat thing to do. But it taught me that it's not a pretty world out there. I can just hear Arnold. "Hey, Cousy is gonna play. What does that mean to me? It means I can get something for me." And if I'm honest about it, in retrospect I probably would have done the same.

Forget about the thirteen years I played for the Celtics. Expediency makes the world go round. At the time, I felt that the thing Auerbach did with me had to be one of the most ludicrous episodes in the history of the league. But that's Arnold.

But Auerbach's emphasis on expediency has served him well. For example, there was the matter of his successor. Prior to the 1965–66 season, Red announced it would be his last. "I'll give them one more shot at me," he growled. The NBA title came down to a seventh game against Los Angeles, but his team pulled it out for him by two points, enabling Red to go out a winner.

Who could possibly follow that act? The Celtics were, by that time, a veteran team. The most important player, Bill Russell, had never played for another professional coach. How would he react to a new guy? We'll never know. Auerbach's brilliant solution as general manager and president was to select as coach the only person he reasoned Bill Russell would play for without a fuss at that stage of his career—Bill Russell.

Red wasn't worried about Xs and Os. He seldom is. His approach is to go to the heart of the problem and try to solve it. No wasted motion. Complete pragmatism. In retrospect, even at the time, the solution to the problem of his successor was obvious. Who better to coach Russell than Russell? Russ's expertise as a coach was completely academic, but he was the most important player, and the only way the Celtics were going to continue the success they had known was to provide Russell with a compatible coach. Auerbach reasoned that Russell calling the shots was the key to continue winning championships. Don't get fancy. Don't look for Bobby Knight types, and don't worry about getting a motivator because Russell wasn't going to be motivated by any outside force. Russell's self-interest as a coach passed all the pressure along to him. I think it was beautiful psychology.

The Celtics didn't win the title that year, despite winning sixty games during the regular season. In the playoffs, they ran into a Philadelphia team having a sensational year. But they came back to win two more championships in 1968 and 1969. So Russ coached three years, and he won two championships. If Red had gone the conventional route, selecting an outside party, where would Russell's motivation have been to win for this guy? In retrospect, what Red did was the only intelligent thing to do. Put the pressure on Russ to prove to the world he could win as a coach as well as a player. As long as he played for himself, Russ was probably going to win. Meanwhile, Auerbach continued to demonstrate that he knows how to win with the least amount of wasted motion in the most pragmatic way.

Much has been made over the years about Auerbach having spawned so many coaches. At one time or another Russell, Sharman, Macauley, Sam Jones, K.C. Jones, Satch, Nelson, Cowens, Loscutoff, I, and many others have coached in both the college ranks and in the NBA. Whatever lessons we drew from Red weren't necessarily technical.

Arnold was an unorthodox coach by today's standards, and even by the old ones. Today's coach is highly structured, disciplined, and organized. College coaches have always had to be that way, the pros less so, at least in the old days.

Arnold was expedient. He just knew how to win. He could appraise talent, he could motivate players, and he was an excellent bench coach. In terms of basic coaching principles, most of us who came through the system were prepared. His was a glorified seat-of-the-pants approach. That's all that was necessary in those days.

Things are different now. Think of Willis Reed. He was made coach of the Knicks and met with moderate success. He really wasn't prepared. Then he went back and volunteered to coach college ball under Lou Carnessecca. He spent time under Atlanta head coach Mike Fratello. He coached for four years at Creighton University. These are people I assume were organized in terms of preparation. Reed should be ready to coach the New Jersey Nets now. None of us were prepared for coaching like that.

— 2 —

More Arnold

RED AUERBACH HAS always preached that contracts or compensation should not be predicated on box scores. He would remember exactly how players contributed, based on what he determined he could rightfully expect from them. I don't know that any of us took that seriously. We moved on the pay scale the way you might expect us to.

One thing Red did as well as possible was find the right player for the right situation. Even though scouting wasn't very sophisticated, and there were only eight or ten teams in the NBA, Red still had more of a choice then than he'd have today, when the league has twenty-five teams and soon will have twenty-seven. You could more easily find the round peg for the round hole back then. Now you might be forced to bang a square peg into the round hole and hope it fits. So Auerbach had better control of his players than coaches enjoy today. In addition, a coach was more inherently autocratic in those days. But you must give Red credit.

Once he got the players, Red exercised little direction

other than gearing some plays to match individual talents. But it was unsophisticated compared with what's going on today. Today's players have defensive keys, offensive keys, motion this, motion that. We had none of that. If we were behind, we pressed. We'd defend and "trap," as they say today, but in a completely unsophisticated way. It was more a question of knowing who you were playing with. If I called a play, it was geared to a specific weakness of an opponent so we could set up Tommy, Ramsey, Sam, or a good shooter. Maybe even Russell had someone he could exploit.

Movement in the transition game was my business. I had certain criteria. If Russell got the rebound in his early days, he was my first thought because he was probably going to try beating his man down the floor. After a while, he would pick his spots. My first choice, in other words, would be the man who had just gotten the rebound or made the steal that set us in motion. Few point guards today think along those lines. Mo Cheeks is, in my mind, the prototypical point guard, and he's one of the few players today who have this thought process. One night last season someone had stolen the ball and Cheeks passed up a guy in the lane who had gotten there quicker to give the ball to the guy who had stolen it. That's just basic psychology. You don't have to go to school to learn it.

Big men who have done the dirty work under the boards and made an effort to run the floor must be rewarded first. You want to reward him not only for the specific act, but also because you want to keep him working at it for the rest of the game. After that, you think about a trailer because then you've got a clear shot or maybe a path to the hoop.

Again, you give it to him at the right time. You can't do it prematurely, because if he has to put the ball to the floor too much he may run into trouble. At least we didn't have to worry as much in those days about a defender stepping in and picking up a charge call. Now every coach in college teaches that maneuver. There are always players reluctant to take the charge, especially if the guy coming in is a center or big forward, but you must be prepared. It's a defensive gamble, and it can be neutralized by giving your man the ball at the last minute.

You could give Dickie Hemrich the ball underneath the basket and he would screw it up somehow. Loscutoff had surprising finesse as a finisher. He was completely sure-handed taking it to the hoop, as well as being effective as far as 18 feet from the basket. I'd pass up Sharman if I had a big guy to go to. If not, and the break didn't develop, I'd dribble back out a little and give it to Sharman behind a pick for a 15-footer that was as good as a layup. You knew your personnel, and after a while everything was done instinctively. The bottom line is that you do what the defense tells you to do.

Red expected us to know how to play basketball. The basic learning was done long before you reached our level. Who had time to teach? Auerbach was the coach, general manager, president, traveling secretary, and anything else we needed. There were no assistant coaches. Now there are as many as four people on the bench for twelve players.

You look back now at some of the things that went on and you might be tempted to label them "primitive." Practices were often bloody. Arnold believed it was a good thing when two of his players came to blows in practice. It kept them "combat ready," especially if they were big guys. I remember Bob Brannum breaking Jack Nichols's nose in practice one day. It was just one of those things. Asserting yourself physically was an absolute must if you were a big guy trying to make one of Red's teams.

Rookies often learned this fact of life the hard way.

We drafted a kid named Frank Mahoney, who was at Brown when I was at Holy Cross. He was an outstanding athlete in both football and basketball, but before he could try to become a professional basketball player he had to go to Korea and get shot at.

When he got out—in either '52 or '53—he came to training camp. After a while, it became evident that Mahoney was a direct threat to Brannum and Bob Harris because he could play and he had come in with such good credentials. They were specialists, more or less, but this kid had a much more well-rounded game.

One day Mahoney came up to me at training camp and said, "What's going on?" Things had gotten rough, and Auerbach never blew the whistle. He lived by the old cliché that there had to be blood before he'd stop it, and then just maybe. Red loved it. The rougher it got, the better he liked it.

BB (Brannum) and Harris took turns guarding Mahoney. Brannum and Harris hammered Mahoney. They put him on the ground. By the end of ten days, two weeks, or whatever, Mahoney would never go to the basket. They hammered him to the floor every time he went in, and Auerbach would never stop it. Arnold might give him the ball out, but he'd never say, "Don't do that" because he was looking for Mahoney to retaliate. The kid wasn't a coward. He just came into a situation, and he was being harassed. For the other two, their livelihood was being threatened. If you were going to take the bread out of their mouths, and their families', you would have to earn it.

Mahoney just said, "What's going on? Don't these guys know we're on the same side?" I remember saying, "Frank, it's every man for himself. You are just going to have to do what's required to make an impact on Auerbach if you're going to make the team."

There was no question in anyone's mind that Mahoney had the talent to make the team, but he never made it out of training camp. I don't know that any of that intimidation goes on today.

It was all so unscientific. As a college coach I was so concerned about utilizing every minute of practice time. We'd have it down to the second. On the professional level it was a lot different.

With Red it was, What does it take to win? Find the talent, get them in shape, keep them motivated, and don't get fancy. That's basically what we did. We didn't change much, once we got the talent. But even before that, those first six years, the practice sessions were the same. Red was out to get us in shape, and he rode herd on us. I don't know if that approach would necessarily work today. You're dealing with much more sophisticated athletes, some with no-cut guarantees in their contracts. The thought never occurred to us to be dissatisfied in any way, other than the normal bitching that goes on. We just went out and got the job done.

Auerbach used to boast about having the toughest training camp in the business. I have no way of comparing. Basically, it meant getting guys in shape and scrimmaging. I think he was smart enough to know that was what the guys preferred, as opposed to structured drill work.

Arnold hated the thought of us associating with players on other clubs. He literally would not let us fraternize or talk to opposing players. The first guy who, I think, violated that policy was Russell. When we went to Philadelphia, Russ visited Wilt Chamberlain. The same was true when Wilt came to Boston. This was in the days when they were friends. Wilt says he hasn't spoken to Russ in twenty years now.

Anyway, that's what Arnold believed in. When I started coaching at Boston College, I tried to act the same way. I remember telling my kids that if they had friends on the other team, not to socialize, especially on the court. I would just as soon you didn't shake hands on the court, I would tell them, although I'm not going to tell you not to. The idea was anything you might do to intimidate an opponent before the game was fair game. If not shaking hands before a game would do it, fine. It wasn't paranoia; it was a strategy. It was just to get the upper hand and steer the flow of intimidation in your direction.

It made sense to me. Any maneuver that would help gain an edge, however minor, I considered valid. The hot locker room, for example, is an old trick of Ben Kerner and Lester Harrison. Do everything possible to intimidate the opposing team before the game. The point is, we weren't supposed to have any social life with opponents at all. Auerbach didn't even want us to talk to them. There'd be situations like we had one year with Rochester, when we must have played them fifteen times in exhibitions, and then played them ten or twelve more times in the regular season. Imagine the leftover hostilities.

People still believe Auerbach is behind every bad thing that happens to them in Boston. If room service is slow, or there is a fire alarm in the hotel at 3:00 in the morning, or even if it rains, there are people in the NBA who believe to this day that Auerbach is behind it. Everything remotely nefarious is attributed to Red. Other people would be offended. Auerbach just takes another puff and smiles.

So there was very little socializing. There was none of this making commercials together, such as Larry Bird and Julius Erving, or Bird and Magic Johnson for Converse. Even your Players' Association contacts were limited. We started the union in '56, but the only meeting was at the All-Star Game. That was the extent of it. We didn't go to Monaco or Bermuda and socialize for two weeks. I don't know what players on other teams were told, but Auerbach did everything possible to alienate us from everyone else in the league.

Another pet peeve of his was what he called "distractions." Even then some of us were interested in what money we could make on the outside, since we surely weren't making an excess of it on the inside. The truth is that winning a championship was a financial drain for a few of us. Devoting an extra month and a half to playing more basketball games actually cost me money. You ask yourself, "What is a championship worth?" For me, playing on six championship teams turned out to be worth it, monetarily. It was translated into dollars, because to this day I'm still exploiting Bob Cousy, whose name grew larger because he played on a championship team six times.

But despite the fact that it worked out for me in the long run, at the time we were very concerned about making money on the outside, simply because we *needed* it. Larry Bird isn't comfortable doing a lot of the outside activities that have been presented to him, and has turned down hundreds of thousands of dollars. He doesn't *need* the money. We did.

What Red wanted, meanwhile, was our undivided attention. He used to scream at us endlessly about outside distractions. "Goddamn it," he would say, "you are getting paid to play this game. Come to practice and for the seven or eight months a year you're here you should be thinking about one thing—the game."

It all seems so silly now, since there weren't really that many things to distract us. Now I go on a trip and pick up the paper to see that a Celtics player will be making a public appearance at noon today, promoting a shoe, or whatever. As time went on, guess who started dabbling in this or that, and had his attention distracted? Arnold J. Auerbach. In some ways, Red can be very flexible. People didn't think he'd ever adjust to agents, but he has. I told you Arnold was expedient to the nth degree.

Red's approach to us was completely basic. I've often heard him say that sometimes he would come into the locker room and not say anything, that in this manner he'd have a greater effect than if he started screaming. I guess everyone who coaches has done that, from time to time, but Red really knew how to utilize that technique.

There were no locker room pep talks, which I think to this day is the right approach at the NBA level. You wind up doing it too often, the other way. The pregame talk was done in a cursory manner. It was, "Hey, this guy can shoot from the key," or, "This guy can't go to his left." It wasn't a game plan. We were just going out to do what we did best.

Arnold retained that simple, direct approach long after he quit coaching. During Heinsohn's tenure, Tommy took sick and had to miss a few games. Red assumed bench duties, backed up by John Killilea, the assistant coach. One night Portland came into town. It was Bill Walton's Boston Garden debut.

Killilea was the scout. At the pregame meeting he put all the usual stuff on the blackboard. There must have been diagrams of ten Portland plays. It was all very impressive. Killilea made his spiel, and then stepped aside. The Master would now speak.

"That's all very nice," Red said, waving his hand at the blackboard. "You want to win the game? Block out on the boards, and play defense!" The Celtics won by twenty-some points. You can look it up.

Auerbach didn't need to have invented something to be known as the man who took full advantage of the idea. What team, for example, is more linked with the concept of the "sixth man" than the Celtics? Everyone assumes Auerbach sat down one day and said, "I'm going to invent the sixth man."

The first true sixth man was probably Ernie Vandeweghe, father of Kiki. When Ernie played for the Knicks, he was a versatile 6'4" player who Joe Lapchick used as a guy to come in and make something happen. The theory hadn't yet been popularized. No one called him the sixth man. He just came into the game.

Auerbach got a lot of mileage from the concept with Frank Ramsey. He was 6'3", and a true two-position player, who was too quick for most forwards of the day and too big for most guards. The idea of having one of your very best players not start the game, but come in as an extra weapon, made sense. In the past, it was assumed that when you came in off the bench you fell off in quality.

The athlete you choose to do this has to meet certain requirements. He can't be a stand-around guy who wants to have the game come to him. You're looking for a guy who can make a steal, grab a rebound, score a basket, and do it quickly. In Ramsey's case, he came out shooting. He had the knack of getting on the scoreboard quickly.

You can't just choose anyone and say, "He is my sixth man." The Celtics were able to capitalize on it for many years. Ramsey. Havlicek. Silas. McHale. Walton. These people were game-changers. I guess the best sixth man today is Michael Cooper, or, at least, he was until this past year. He embodies the two-position guy, he can make a steal, he can hit the three-pointer. He has many ways to change the game.

Red didn't have a monopoly on toughness. The league was a different enterprise back then. No one survived underneath without being tough. There was a code, and we all were forced to live by it. Arnold certainly never had any trouble adapting to it.

Guards were wary of setting picks. Even in Old-

Timers' Games I'd set picks with one hand up covering my face. They used to try to clip you, and you don't forget those things.

I'll never forget the time Loscy nailed Terry Dischinger while he was setting a pick in Boston. Loscy wasn't guarding Terry. Dischinger was on top of the key, and Loscy was guarding the man behind him. Terry was setting the pick on Loscy when Loscy slid in between them while following his man. As he did he caught Dischinger and shattered his nose. Blood was everywhere. The guy hit the floor and was in shock. He wasn't unconscious, but he probably wished he was.

All this happened so quickly. It was a graphic demonstration of what went on between those big guys. Sometimes we guards would get caught in the crossfire. That's the way Red wanted the game played. If people thought they could casually set picks, they would have an advantage. Your man could score, and that's a big negative. The biggest insult of all was to have a basket result from a little guy waltzing in and setting a pick.

So the easiest way is to be direct and just wipe out the little guy as aggressively as possible. Either he would never go in there again, or, if he did, he'd be tentative. I guess all the old jocks tell war stories about how tough it was, but there is no question it was far, far wilder than the game today. Arnold felt quite comfortable.

Incidentally, there was an early clue from Larry Bird that he was a throwback who would have fared well with Auerbach, the coach. The Celtics were playing an exhibition game against Indiana in the Market Square Arena during Bird's rookie season. Late in the game Bird absolutely flattened Indiana guard Jerry Sichting. People naturally speculated that this was some carry-over from the collegiate rivalry between Sichting's Purdue team and Bird's Indiana State squad. Purdue was highly embarrassed when Indiana State annihilated them while Bird was in uniform.

But Bird quickly set the record straight. "I just didn't want some guard setting a pick on me," he explained. If Auerbach wasn't already in love with Bird, he surely was ready to adopt him after hearing that.

Auerbach's relationship with the players as individuals was limited. It amounted to barking loudly in public, which allows him to say to this day how tough he was. But within the unit he was often a pussycat. We used to pull practical jokes on him all the time. He would put up with this to a point, and then he would explode. I might be the ringleader, but he wouldn't bark at me directly. He'd go off in a general tantrum, with a lot of four-letter words. That would do for the next three or four weeks, until there was another buildup. It's not unlike what we do with our own kids. They get away with a lot of stuff, up to a point. We blow up, and the process begins all over again.

Often, if the incident involved Russ or myself Red would spend two or three weeks making up, which would have the effect of neutralizing me. It's all a very interesting study.

Arnold didn't spend a lot of time talking to anyone among the players. He didn't have any confidants. I got closer to him than the others because we made more than one trip overseas together during the off-season. Just by virtue of spending that much time together in foreign countries, we inevitably grew closer.

After five or six years, Auerbach kind of made me privy to what was going on. In December 1955 he told me that he had Russ, the guy who was going to change everything. Maybe some of this had to do with me being the team captain, but he did tell me things. Other than that, it was, "Goddamn it. Just get the job done!" Maybe there were players who sifted through the routine—show up for practice, get the job done—and felt closer to him, but I doubt it. If you didn't get the job done, he was going to scream at you.

Of course, on a professional level, what coach has time to develop relationships like you would on a college level, where you get more involved in a player's academic life, his love life, and his personal problems. Arnold never demonstrated any such interest with regard to his players. When did he have the time? As I said, he was the general manager, the president, the traveling secretary. He didn't even have time to get chummy.

Arnold liked to think he handled everybody in the same way. He had one gear. I don't want to say that Russell and I got special handling because we never really took advantage of the situation. Even Russ. He didn't like to practice, but no one else was offended by that. Auerbach was always smart enough to understand the difference he had with his superstars, as opposed to the transients. He also knew how to handle the guys who needed a fire lit under them, guys like Brannum, Loscutoff, and Heinsohn. He knew who needed a boost and who didn't.

I would come in and be so uptight I certainly didn't want him to scream at me to motivate me. I would have gone out there overprepared emotionally. Heinsohn was the perennial whipping boy. We all got on Tommy's case.

Once Russ and Tommy and Ramsey came, and we turned the corner from being an also-ran to the team with the hammer, Red's challenge was to handle this wide range of personalities and find a way to keep us fresh and motivated. As I said, there wasn't much need for strategy.

Motivation was no small task. Some coaches don't really believe this. I find their attitudes difficult to understand. In a team sport, you have to motivate everybody.

Tom Landry has obviously been a very successful

football coach, but I remember him saying a long time ago that emotion and motivation rank very low on his scale of important aspects of coaching. He felt that as long as he did the preparation during the week, his players were pros and would bring their own emotion to the game. I remember thinking, "My word, if I were the owner and I read that, I'd get rid of that guy fast."

Well, Landry has been so successful. But how much more successful do you think the Dallas Cowboys could have been? With the talent they had, they probably should have won more than two Super Bowls. How many years did we hear, "Dallas can't win the big one"? For a guy to feel that strongly about the lack of need for the emotional complement to the physical talents strikes me as sad. He is missing the point.

Arnold dealt with a wide range of personalities, and he always had his hand on the tiller. Looking back, it's amazing what he accomplished with those All-Star egos. You'd think there might be frequent eruptions, but that was not the case.

The only occasional rumbling came from Arnold himself. He did it whenever he thought it was necessary. I've watched the Celtics undergo some marked highs and lows over the past two seasons, and sometimes the lows really overwhelm them. There is tremendous fluctuation in effort, especially on the road.

We had these dips in our time. Auerbach used to sense it, time it right, and scream at us to get us going. Now, player-coach relationships have changed, particularly the leverage a player has, as opposed to 25 years ago. But Arnold's timing on his outbursts always had the desired impact and succeeded in reawakening our competitive juices. We were always motivated by an undercurrent of fear, which seldom exists today, and when you complement that with Auerbach's well-timed outbursts, it created the proper effect. Today a coach could approach the situation in the same way—the same temperament, the same screaming—and it might not work the same way at all. In fact, it's safe to say it probably would be completely inappropriate and ineffective. Today's coach wouldn't have the same amount of control and the same impact on players as Arnold did.

What made Auerbach's approach so fascinating was the fact that for fourteen years he answered to a man with a temperament nothing at all like his. Walter Brown had a temper, but after he blew off steam he was a gentleman. They were almost a good cop–bad cop pair. You had kindly Walter and blustery Arnold. Walter didn't have much money, and Red made sure he kept what he had. One thing about Red. He has always been a good financial watchdog for his owners.

In the old days we weren't squired around in buses. We walked, if possible, or we took cabs. We'd get to a town and take cabs from the airport to the hotel. When you got there you went to Red for reimbursement. Red felt he knew exactly what the fare was from every destination in the league to every other destination, and his word on what the trip *should* have cost was law. And he chiseled for every penny. You'd think it was his money. I guess to Red it was.

As a general manager, Red has always been out of the George Halas school, where the nickels are tossed around, as they say, like manhole covers. At the time I received my offer to coach the Cincinnati Royals, I also discussed the possibility of coaching the Celtics. I didn't really expect Red to match the Royals' offer, which was for $100,000. But being offered less than half that to coach the Celtics was sobering, I must say.

Being a general manager, to Arnold, meant acting as a player personnel director. It didn't mean doing anything to drum up interest in the team other than to put one on the floor. To this day, Arnold thinks promotion and marketing means putting a team on the floor, period. He always objected to the promotions other teams put on. I agree with him, to a point. In St. Louis, Ben Kerner would bring in the big bands. I think you've got to sell basketball, but if you rely on Count Basie to bring in people, you've got to have Count Basie all the time.

One of the greatest things Auerbach has been able to perpetuate is the idea that if you are an older player, or perhaps even something of a misfit by other people's standards, there may very well be a home for you in Boston. It's one thing to say that Red was placing round pegs in round holes when he took a Carl Braun, a Don Nelson, a Wayne Embry, a Pete Maravich, a Bill Walton, or even a Dennis Johnson, but you still have to know that players can function in terms of what you want them to do.

In other words, a Carl Braun or a Pete Maravich on a weaker team might have been self-destructive. At some point in his career a player who once had certain skills just can't carry a team any longer. Arnold has always recognized the type of player who can function on a strong team but not a weak one. To be successful he must go to a team that has enough strength to take the pressure off him.

A guy thinks, "Hey, not only am I now a Celtic, but I've got a chance to win a championship." The time has come again for the Celtics to find one of those guys.

Red is not always easy to live with, and some players who passed through the Celtics have never accommodated themselves to his personal style. One former teammate has confided in me that if he's in Boston he doesn't even want to go to Red's office. He just doesn't like Red's general demeanor. You come in and it's "Hey, what do *you* want?" Red feels he has to have the upper hand. He wants to put you on the defensive. Most of us can ignore it; it's just his way. But a few can't.

It's that type of behavior that has unendeared him, shall we say, to most of the rest of the league. He has built, through whatever means, an enduring monument, which is ironic, in a way.

We all felt a closeness to Walter Brown. If he were alive, all the nice things people say about the Celtics would tie in so nicely. Walter Brown was a great sportsman, a humanitarian, and just a beautiful man. We were all close to him, Auerbach included. Everything would have fit.

The reality is that Arnold has persevered, and the Celtics have kept winning. Auerbach thinks it's him. Chance has surely played a role, but for the most part, I agree with him. The guy has come up with the players.

— 3 —

Bill Russell
on the Court

WE STRUGGLED ALONG for six years without great success. Macauley, Sharman, and I were All-Stars, but the Celtics weren't on the same level as Minneapolis or even New York. George Mikan dominated the inside game in those days. With him, the Minneapolis Lakers won five championships between 1949 and 1954.

Our problem was that we were a running team that didn't have the ball often enough to run. Macauley was a fine scorer in the middle, but he wasn't robust enough to be a superior rebounder. He could block shots occasionally, but overall he was a finesse player who specialized in offense. We lacked that extra ingredient in the middle that could put us over the top.

During the 1955–56 season, Auerbach told me he had found the man, the answer. The player he had in mind was Bill Russell, who was then leading the University of San Francisco to a second consecutive NCAA championship. These were innocent times. Today, Alonzo Mourning blocks a few shots in high school and every basketball fan in America hears about it. Back

31

then, Bill Russell was in the process of revolutionizing basketball, and millions of people who professed to love the sport were blissfully ignorant of that fact. So when Red Auerbach told me he'd found the player of our dreams, my basic reaction was, "That's nice. We'll see how he does in training camp."

I had no idea Auerbach was talking about a man unlike anyone I had ever seen. Red was right. Bill Russell *was* The Answer. Without Bill Russell there wouldn't be any Celtic Mystique.

I really don't have a clear recollection of the first time I saw Russell play. He had come to Boston directly from the 1956 Olympics in Melbourne, where he had led the U.S. team to the gold medal. We were doing all right even before he came. Tommy Heinsohn had been our first draft pick, and he was playing very well. Frank Ramsey was back from the army. Jungle Jim Loscutoff was in his second year. Sharman and I were well established. We had a veteran named Arnie Risen to play center. When Russell arrived, we were in first place in the Eastern Division of the 8-team league, with a record of 16 wins and 8 losses.

There was a press conference. I remember that. We were playing St. Louis on, I believe, a Saturday afternoon. The game itself was very close, and we were able to pull it out in the end when Macauley (whom we had traded to St. Louis, along with Cliff Hagan, for the rights to Russell) outsmarted himself, enabling me to slip Heinsohn a backdoor pass for a game-winning basket. As I recall, I was going to pass the ball to Heinsohn in the corner. Macauley smelled it out and led me to believe he was going for the steal. I just made eye contact with Tommy, and, fortunately, he got my drift. It was a simple back door play. Heinsohn laid it in, and that's what I remember about the game.

Russell? I remember our reaction to Russ was that

he didn't score much at all. He looked uncertain with himself offensively and in simple ballhandling. But there was no question he was going to be a force, at least in our minds, on the backboards. He was what we needed to complete the puzzle. It was just what Arnold had been saying for months. I don't know if Russell blocked any shots that day, and whatever offensive prowess he would demonstrate never came through that day.

We were in first place, and we weren't thinking about an NBA championship. We knew we were competitive, and that we had a good chance to get to the Finals. Russell topped it off, in our minds. I remember how quickly he assimilated himself into whatever was going on out there on the floor. He became an immediate force, a meaningful factor, and he started to get as much playing time as the rest of us were getting. He wasn't necessarily picking up the plays all that quickly, but on his own he picked up our individual idiosyncrasies and made the appropriate adjustments. It seems like this might be easy to do, but it's not. You sit there. You study who you are going to play and immediately know how you are going to adjust, or how you are going to play him the next time. Russell always did this quickly, and he seldom repeated any meaningful mistakes.

Oh, Russell could get lazy like the rest of us. For example, he would let Clyde Lovelette hit three, four, or even five outside shots in a row until Arnold would call time out and say, "For Chrissake. Will you just go out there and extend three or four feet and guard that son of a bitch?" Russ would pick his spots, just like the rest of us. It is human nature.

People know vaguely about how Russell literally ran a good player out of the league, but the story has faded with time. The poor guy was Neil Johnston.

Neil was a 6'8" center from Ohio State. He had a square jaw and a funny half-hook, half-runner shot that was accurate enough to make him the league's leading scorer for three consecutive seasons. By the time Russ came along, Johnston was a little past his prime, but the Philadelphia Warriors weren't in the market for a replacement. Neil Johnston was still a respected player in the league.

Neil couldn't jump. His shot had a line drive trajectory. He was not agile in terms of his faking. He wasn't that smooth. He wasn't, shall we say, a "modern" player. He was ideal for Russell's talents.

Johnston used to step into the basket, unlike Bob Houbregs, who was famous for his hook but who used to fade away from the basket. Neil would fake right, and not take a drop step as we know today, but would instead step toward the basket. Russ was lefthanded and Neil was righthanded. He was shooting right into that left hand.

Right from the start, Russ didn't even have to jump to block Johnston's shot. He would be there quicker than poor Neil. Neil went from being scoring champion to being out of the league. In short order. Neil Johnston not only couldn't play his game against Bill Russell, he also couldn't play it against *anybody*. It was incredible the effect Bill Russell had on a man who had been such a scoring machine.

Neil couldn't adjust. He had no other weapon. He did not have an accurate outside shot. All his work was done inside and for his entire career he had been effective against every other center in the league—Mikan, Larry Foust, all of them. Now he was up against a new force in Bill Russell and he didn't have the talent to adjust. How could he adjust? He couldn't play forward, in my opinion. He had no outside shot whatsoever. He didn't run particularly well. I don't remember him making many layups. All Neil had was that one shot.

If you're a good hitter and some guy comes up with a pitch you can't hit, that's got to work on you. The ball gets smaller and smaller, and that's what happened to Neil. It was incredible for Russell to have that kind of impact on a player of Johnston's stature.

In talking about Bill Russell and his impact on the game of basketball more than 30 years after he entered the NBA and 20 years after he departed, one thing remains clear: there has never been anything like him, before or since.

I remember walking into a hockey game, never having been to one since I had come to Boston. The only name I knew was Gordie Howe. It was obvious who Gordie Howe was. Comparing him to the others was like comparing night to day. Bill Russell had that kind of impact on basketball. Chamberlain was more mechanical. I can remember looking at Chamberlain and saying that he was going to be a force. But Russell was far more fluid and graceful.

There is virtually no comparison between Russell and all the centers who had come before him. The only smaller player who even remotely compared was Jim Pollard, the fine forward for the Lakers. Pollard was 6'5", and he had jumping ability and grace. He was very much a "modern" player. However, he played a different position. No center was anything like Russell, and I'm not even sure Pollard is an apt comparison.

The centers of the day were big, cumbersome guys. Some were more agile than others, but Russell was a complete departure. He was quick and agile, and he could play far off the man he was guarding. I see Bird do that now, incidentally. He will lash out with his arm like a snake and steal the ball. Bird does it to players who have every reason to think they are quicker than he is, but that's another story. Russell always *was* quicker than the man he was guarding.

He would play off his guy, but have the quickness to surprise anybody, especially penetrators. Time and again Russell fooled people. They might know Russell was coming, but *how* did he get there so quickly? He would just flash in there. I thought Patrick Ewing would have this kind of power, and for the first time this past season I saw him do things like Russell did. But Russell was able to stop penetrating shooters from the beginning. Once he established this fact, with consistent results, it was no longer a surprise. Then it became *intimidation*. Now he had true impact on the other team's offense because every potential penetrator was thinking, "Where is Russell going to come from?"

I recall hearing the phrase so many times: *Russell came out of nowhere!* You always had that feeling about Russell. He had the God-given talent to play this type of defense and the determination to want to do it.

I first saw the effect his defense had on an opponent with Macauley. In his first two or three years, Macauley was actually a fairly effective shot blocker. Something happened after his third year. He stopped blocking shots and started worrying about his man, period. Either someone said something to him—possibly Arnold—or he responded to the reaction from the fans. In those days, we were dealing with less sophisticated fans and a far less sophisticated media. They were watching a guy trying to help out on defense and thinking, "This guy's man is scoring, and he's nowhere near him. What's going on?" It's not that Macauley was insecure, either. It's just that at some point he started thinking, "I am going to take care of mine, and you are going to take care of yours." He stopped helping out. I know it affected me in that I knew it and I was a little more reluctant to gamble outside.

In Russell's case, during the seven years I played with him, you *always* knew he was going to be there backing you up. And I was vulnerable against certain types of players.

One of those guys was Richie Guerin. He would try to take me inside. I'd say, "You big bully, get out of here." I used to talk to him and talk to him because Richie was 6'4" and strong. I would immediately go over to Russ and say, "Look, hey, help me out." I would try to front Richie, knowing full well that Russ was back there, and he would either reject the shot or blast Richie once or twice, and that would get him out. Richie would go back outside, where I thought he belonged. Russell could always be depended upon.

Russell never showboated with his blocked shots—never. He always had the touch. That's the game he brought to the Celtics. I never remember him making loud rejects for the sake of getting someone's attention. How long should it take any effective shot blocker to say to himself, "What is the sense of blocking the shot out of bounds?" So few of them get this into their heads. The object is to regain possession for your team, not to send the ball into the twentieth row. We have a good shot blocker now in Kevin McHale. It's rare when he knocks the ball out of bounds. To me it's very simple. If you're the best shot blocker in the league, what sense does it make merely to knock the ball out of bounds? Russell always had it figured out.

People ask how good Russell was on offense. The answer is he was good enough to average 16 points a game for a 13-year career. I used to kid him and say, "You can't hit a bull in the ass," and in fact he couldn't. We talked about his superb touch in blocking shots and controlling the basketball. On offense he had no touch from the outside—at least, it didn't seem that way. Now I would not hesitate to give him the ball at the end of a fast break. He not only had the hands and the ability to finish off, but you could also throw the ball as high as you wanted to. You could do it in a variety of ways, and he could go get it. He was extremely versatile. You didn't even have to be on target with the pass. So in terms of transition, he was ideal. Obviously, you don't need a shooting touch for that.

Eventually, he taught himself to play some offense, and we did come up with the "six" (his uniform number) play for him. We'd clear out the left side and allow him to drive past his opponent. After a while, people began to respect him on the drive, and he came up with the ability to make the 15-footer. I don't know his shooting percentage, but it was enough to keep them honest.

His best individual shot was a little hook, which wasn't a bad shot for him. By the end of my career—which would make it his seventh year—you could go to Russell for points. If you needed something from him, especially if it was a guy he could really exploit, and you went to him with a degree of regularity, he would produce the eighteen or twenty or whatever it was you needed. It wasn't so much he had produced the shooting *touch* as it was that he had developed the moves to the basket for high percentage shots. He would *never* take a bad shot. He was reluctant to take a low percentage shot and look bad doing it. But once Russell established his offensive confidence, he was always able to create high percentage shots.

Russell's one slight area of difficulty was handling the ball in close quarters. He had some problems there. He wasn't that adept at putting the ball on the floor and disengaging himself if necessary. I would be more apt to run a pick-and-roll with Heinsohn. But Russell was totally unconcerned about his offense, anyway. He was only interested in the context of exploiting someone. Even then, it was a question of saving it until we needed it.

One of our favorite tactics was what we now know as the alley oop. I used to love those things. I'd save it for maybe twice a game. Maybe just once. If it was a good opponent, we might save it until the end of the game, and use it when we needed it. If it was not a good opponent, maybe we'd use it when we were up by twenty. It was an easy basket with Russell on the receiving end.

With Russell being able to jump so much higher and being much more agile than everyone else, the alley oop was always there when we wanted it. I suspect that's the way the Bulls feel today with Michael Jordan on their side. I remember loving to come out and working the alley oop because it was successful almost every time. Half the time, given Russ's speed advantage, he was standing there waiting. You didn't even have to put it that high. In those days, the alley oop was considered to be a truly spectacular play.

As a passer, Russell progressed from bad to good, and of course he was a brilliant outlet passer. In the halfcourt, he wasn't particularly creative. But on the outlet, he was the best. Russ could turn in midair and release the ball even before he hit the ground. When it came to the long outlet, he could put some muscle behind it and get it to you strong, with accuracy.

With all of his finesse, Russell was still not a player you'd care to challenge. He didn't play a muscle game. He didn't play a finesse game. He never provoked anyone, the way Bird sometimes will today. He would retaliate, but he would never be the physical aggressor.

Russell had athletic strength, as opposed to body-building strength. He was so much quicker than everyone else that he seldom got into a physical thing. No one wanted to get close to him because they knew he would run by them. Under the boards, Russell had a sense of position, and that great jumping ability. Early in his career, especially, when he used to run the floor much more than he did later on, opponents were reluctant to hang in there with him. Players forgot about the offensive rebound because they knew if they didn't have a three or four-foot head start, Russell would blow by them. I used to look for Russell sneaking away all the time. If we didn't get him two or three transition hoops like that, I was disappointed.

When the situation arose, Russell could take care of himself. He wasn't like Gene Conley, who got into fights all the time. The greatest heavyweight fights I have ever seen were Gene Conley and any number of opponents. Gene is a nice gentle guy to this day, but on the floor he was exceptionally combative. He would whack people.

This never happened with Russell. Well, almost never. There was a night in the Providence Arena, where we used to play a lot of home-away-from-home games. We were playing the Lakers, who had a center named Jim Krebs. There was a jam between Krebs and Russell, and suddenly the left arm of Bill Russell came out of nowhere. It looked like Russ's arm was a snake. It somehow wound its way through a crowd of people. It finally reached its destination and caught Krebs coming in.

The game ended almost simultaneously. They carried Krebs off. He was unconscious. The locker rooms at that old arena were situated in such a way that there was a door in between a little room that the trainer used and the locker room. I went into the trainer's room and Krebs was just coming out of it. I'd gone in to ask about something or another, and I just happened to be in there as he came to.

The trainer was still working on Krebs, who had a wide-open cut on his forehead, and Krebs was mumbling, "What happened? What possibly hit me?" He had absolutely no idea what hit him, or how, or anything. He had been knocked unconscious far longer than a ten count. I think after that people got to thinking, "Why piss Russell off?"

Auerbach had always ingrained in us that statistics are meaningless, and for the most part people who played for the Celtics had bought it. But Russell embodied this philosophy more than anyone ever had, at least anyone with that level of ability. It's funny: A record I held for a long time was the single-game assist mark. I had twenty-eight in a game against Minneapolis in 1959, and one of the oddities of that game was that Russell was injured and couldn't play. But everything we threw up that day went in, and when it was all over we had beaten the Lakers by a 173–139 score, setting records in both team high and combined scores. Those records lasted for a long, long time.

I've had to tell people over the years that, to me, it was a meaningless record. What's the big deal in getting 28 assists in a game like that? If you get 12 meaningful assists in a playoff game, that's more important. Russell understood this better than anyone.

Bill Russell responded to the moment. The only play we ever set up for him was that "six" play. Everything else just came off the flow. We always felt his offense was there any time he wanted it. Any time he wanted to beat his man down the floor, he did.

Russell was there for one reason—to win the basketball game. He may have done things for effect off the floor but never while playing the game. He wouldn't dunk in warmups. It had nothing to do with winning the game. As time went on and dunking became more and more fashionable, and teams had a half a dozen guards who could slam it through, it used to get to me a little. Russell would never respond to any of that. I used to think to myself, "Let's blow the whistle, and we'll show them how to play this game without having to dunk the ball." We didn't have any leapers. Even Sam Jones wasn't a leaper. K.C. wasn't a leaper. In the earlier days, Don Barksdale was. At this time Russell was the only one who could really get up there. But he held unnecessary dunking in disdain, the same way he disdained shooting for the sake of amassing individual points, as opposed to shooting for the sake of accomplishing the central purpose—winning the basketball game.

The one occasionally sticky area was practice. To be blunt, Bill Russell was not a practice player. He was never enthusiastic about practice. In the early years, he wasn't necessarily reluctant to participate, but by the late stages of my career we would say, "Russ, go sit in the stands." He just wouldn't take practice seriously.

Russell played long minutes. We knew when the games started that Russell was prepared to play as long and as hard as necessary to win. It didn't make sense that he should bust his ass in practice when he was going to play forty-four minutes per game. I never remember resenting the fact that Russell didn't want to practice. In fact, the only thing that bothered me is when he used to screw around when we wanted to get something constructive done.

But eleven championships in thirteen seasons proves rather dramatically that Bill Russell was a good game player.

— 4 —

Bill Russell
off the Court

THE MEMORY OF Bill Russell, the player, may need to be revived a bit by old-timers like me, but Bill Russell, the public personality, is very much with us today. Since retiring in 1969, Russell has never been far from the public eye. He coached the Seattle Supersonics in the mid-seventies. He coached the Sacramento Kings for a little over half a season last year and is currently in their front office. He has dabbled in newpaper writing, and worked for many years as a basketball broadcaster for ABC, CBS, and TBS.

Bill Russell is a larger-than-life personality. And I suppose there is no other way to put it than to say he is a larger-than-life black personality. He has always been forthright, and some would go so far as to call him militant. I'm not so sure he's not just Bill Russell.

I have on my mantel a clock with an inscription reading "May the next seventy be as pleasant as the last seven. To the Cousys from your friends, the Russells." I mention this because Russ has a proclivity for making radical-sounding statements, looking for dramatic impact.

"I hate all whites."

"Boston is the most bigoted city in the United States."

"I'd rather be in jail in Sacramento than mayor of Boston."

Is Russell acting? Is he sincere? Is he just generally committed to pulling the establishment's chain? Does everything come down to race and what he believes are whites' perceptions of blacks? Does he think about the impact of what he's saying at all?

Look at the job Russell did in Seattle, the broadcast work he's done, and his last coaching job in Sacramento. Is it possible he just took what I like to call the path of least resistance in those jobs? Russell never had any insecurity problems as a player—he just showed up and dominated. As a broadcast analyst, he didn't put in the time to prepare. He assumed he was going to show up and dominate, I guess. He relied on his instincts. He had the same approach as a coach in Seattle and Sacramento, in terms of practice habits and the like. Jocks are notoriously lazy in nonathletic endeavors. They're spoiled and pampered, especially superstars. They expect to be waited on and to receive a great deal of money for doing as little as possible.

Before trying to explain what it was like dealing with Bill Russell, I'd better outline my basic philosophy. I have always felt that bigotry in any form is the world's primary problem. Everything flows from our inability since Adam and Eve to live harmoniously with our neighbors for a wide range of reasons, the greatest of which, in my opinion, is insecurity.

Minority and majority have perpetually fought. There is always a minority to put down because people reason that if we give "them" the same opportunities we have, they may rise up and take what we value away from us. I couldn't relate to this idea at any point in my life, not growing up in New York, not in high school, and not in college, where the topic for my senior thesis was the persecution of minority groups.

I am capable of hating selectively. I just never understood how basic reason and common sense allow you to jump from hating an individual to hating everyone who resembles him or her.

I came very close to giving up my Catholic religion over the issue of segregated churches in the South. I felt the height of religious hypocrisy was telling me since I reached the age of reason that God's basic tenet was the equality of man while, at the same time, allowing segregated churches. I couldn't cope with this.

I have also found that some of the biggest bigots I know are members of minorities themselves who have experienced persecution. Yet this is understandable. There's a reason for insecurity in these cases, and I allow them that opinion.

I do not allow that same privilege to the clergy. They have committed their lives to serving God and His creatures, regardless of any differences, and to do otherwise is to live a complete lie. Despite my feelings, I try to avoid grandstanding. To be honest, maybe it has never been in my best interests to be active publicly or get up on a soapbox, although I have made an attempt to do so by example. I became a life member of the NAACP in the early sixties, a decision that related to some degree to my relationship with Russ.

I wrote a few articles for national magazines in the early seventies shooting down the stupid myths kept alive by generations of bigots that blacks can't function under pressure—can't handle positions of athletic responsibility such as quarterback—implying that blacks can function instinctively in sports but not intellectually. I think this is what Isiah Thomas was referring to in the aftermath of the Rodman–Bird controversy two years ago.

I have also been active in the Big Brothers program, both on a local level in the fifties and on the national level in the sixties and seventies. It is a very worthwhile program for fatherless boys, and now there is a comparable program for young girls called the Big Sisters.

During that time I acted as a Big Brother to three different youngsters in Worcester, Mass., each for two to three years. Two of those boys were black. Other than making a subtle statement, I felt that since Worcester did not have a very large black community, black youngsters who needed help would be harder to place.

In any event, I have always felt very strongly about this issue, and perhaps, therefore, my observations regarding Bill Russell's motives and how the race issue plays a role in American sports can be viewed more objectively. I have never been a crusader, but I have never been reluctant to stand up and be counted.

The question is, has Bill Russell used race as a cop-out? What about his continual refusal to sign autographs? Is there a tie-in?

First of all, no jocks ever *like* to sign autographs. Jocks just don't like to be role models for kids. They want to *be* kids. Jocks, in general, are lazy and undisciplined and shun responsibility. Maybe society's bigotry is giving Russell an excuse. How many pro athletes go from sports to a comparable level of achievement in other areas? It happens, but it is seldom done. Maybe we are just following a pattern. Maybe Russell is just following a pattern, but it is easier to use the race issue to explain what he does. What I am trying to say is that maybe Bill Russell is just a sorehead.

The older I get, the less patient I am with people. I have always wanted my privacy, but I used to have a lot more patience. Now I have less, especially in large groups. I still put myself in those situations because that's the way I earn a living. It's a pain in the ass to me, but it's worth the effort. Russ has always been, in that sense, truer to himself than I have been.

It's been twenty years since Russell played in Boston. Nothing new "bad" has happened to him that I know of. Every time he comes to Boston, people try to make up to him. The people sitting in the stands now are the children of the older bigots. Some may be new to the area and have no idea what went on thirty years ago, when Russell was suffering ridiculous racial slights. He is very proud and he has adopted a stoic and militant image for the public. I think if he were offered a way to extricate himself from this image without losing face, he might very well do so. But how do you do that after years of establishing your position? I don't know whether he would really start signing autographs, but it is obviously more inconvenient and a larger pain in the ass trying to explain to everyone why you're *not* signing autographs than it is to scribble your name. Ted Williams put himself into a similar corner by not tipping his cap for the last years of his career.

Maybe Russ will change someday. When he brought the Kings to Boston in January of 1988, he was given a tremendous ovation. Everyone was watching him to see if he would acknowledge the crowd. It was a long, long ovation, and he finally acknowledged it. That's a first, as far as I can remember.

As respectful as you can and should be about Russell's private feelings about race, it's not always easy to translate that passion into a justification for downright rude behavior. There is one incident illustrating this side of Russell that I will never forget.

In 1963, a bunch of us were touring Eastern Europe. We might have been in Romania. We might have been in Yugoslavia. I don't remember the name of the town, but I clearly recall the look of the hotel. Despite being the best in town, it reminded me of Count Dracula's castle.

The dining room had a hardwood floor, and there was a dance floor in the center. One night, we were in the dining room. It was quite late, and there weren't many other guests left. The violinist was doing his thing, and there was hardly anyone else in the dining room except a well-dressed elderly couple at the other end of the room.

At some point in the meal the lady got up. She was in her sixties, maybe even seventies, and she was wearing fur. She looked very elegant. I was facing her. Russ was across from me. She came all the way across the room, heels clicking on the hardwood floor. She stood behind Russ and made a speech about how she and her husband were from Boston. She had been a fan for years. "Would you, Bill, sign this menu?" she asked.

Now, when you're overseas, it becomes more intimate when you meet someone from back in the States. This is especially true in a setting such as Romania or Yugoslavia. It creates a bond of some substance. She made her speech and Russell never stopped eating. He never looked up. Obviously, it was a very uncomfortable situation.

Here is this elderly woman who must have needed a certain amount of courage to walk across that large room and make an impassioned speech to these jocks. And here was Russell ignoring her.

Jerry Lucas, who was sitting next to Russ, jumped right up, grabbed the menu from the lady, and said, "Ma'am, why don't I get all the boys to sign this for you, and I'll bring it back to the table?" This allowed the lady to depart with dignity; otherwise, she might still be standing there over Russ.

I know a white can't appreciate the reaction of Bill Russell, or of any proud black, until he or she can jump into black skin. For a brush with racism as practiced by blacks against whites, I think back to a time when I was connected with the ABC Superstars. We worked out of the Bahamas for three years, and I learned a lot about discrimination. I don't know how it is now, but in the early eighties the climate was hostile toward whites. The feeling may even have been more anti-American than antiwhite in general, but, at any rate, it was tied to race.

On a number of occasions I would come in with Bill Russell and the black porters would grab his bags and leave mine sitting there. O.J. Simpson was among the prominent black Americans with us, and he was treated very well. The locals would really put themselves out for the black athletes. It was obvious they were catering to the blacks while leaving the whites on their own. That was healthy, as far as I was concerned, in that it gave whites a taste of their own medicine. It pissed me off, but in terms of appreciating what Bill Russell must have felt at times back home, despite the fact that he was a star, it was very enlightening.

It showed me the effect racial bigotry can have on your psyche. Some people say when they hear about a famous black athlete suffering a racial slight, "What is he complaining about? Look at all the money he makes." Money, of course, has nothing to do with anything.

While all this was going on in the Bahamas, Russ was still Russ. One day I was standing with Russ waiting for our bags, and a lady approached us. Unfortunately, she asked Russ first for his autograph. As soon as she did I knew I was going to have to deal with a problem. I knew what his response would be. He said, "I'm sorry;

I don't sign," or whatever. Then she turned to me. Now, in this situation, I am either a bad guy or a bad guy. On the one hand, I am going to make him look bad, on the other I am going to have to compromise my own integrity by not signing. I quickly signed. But what do you do in a case like that?

Russell just doesn't seem to care how he makes people feel, not only those he rejects, however politely, but those who happen to be with him at the time. Here is another Superstars story. This time it was Super Teams, and we were at the Sheraton Waikiki during the late seventies. They had roped off a patio dining area outside for the Super Teams people and had a private buffet line set up there.

One morning, the line was full of jocks. Los Angeles Dodgers pitcher Tommy John came over. He is an awfully nice guy and a big basketball fan. He chatted among the tables for a while, and then Russell came down the stairs. I was going through the buffet line, and chatting with Russell. While we were talking, Tommy John came over with the menu. "Would you please sign this?" he asked. But he made the mistake of saying it so everyone in the immediate area could hear it. Talk about embarrassment. Russ said, "I'm sorry. I don't sign."

You can't condone some of these things. You've *got* to make exceptions. Tommy John is such a nice man. Tommy said, "I'm sorry. I didn't know you don't sign." He walked away with his tail between his legs. I could have cried for the poor man. I don't know what it all means. Can you handle it better, or is your anger so intense you don't see anything, anyone, or anything that is white?

I like to think I'm not naive about what Russell has experienced. The Celtics were the first team to sign a black player, and that was six years before Russ joined the club. Chuck Cooper was a 6'6" forward from Duquesne University. Arnold signed him the same year I became a Celtic. It didn't take long for me to learn what discrimination was all about, at least vicariously.

We were playing an exhibition in the South. I believe it was Charlotte, N.C. They wouldn't let Coop stay in the same hotel with us. There were no other accommodations, so Coop and I just left right after the game and took a train back to New York. Coop had grown up in Pittsburgh, and this was his first exposure to the Jim Crow mentality. We didn't even talk about it on that trip. I was so embarrassed and felt so bad for Coop.

I was embarrassed to be white. Even growing up in what is presumed to be a ghetto environment, Coop was a very articulate, sensitive guy, and it was difficult to imagine a man like this having to put up with such treatment. He had never been faced with that type of indignity.

To Auerbach's everlasting credit, race was never handled on the Celtics as if it was a "problem." The team had twelve basketball players, as opposed to three black players and nine whites. We didn't think in terms of color. Now you do, much more so, because the league is about seventy-five percent black, and the issue is the presence of white players, not vice versa. The percentage has been reversed. But on the Celtics we never thought of it in the context of color.

We didn't think in racial terms, and as a result, when I was faced with an incident like the one in Charlotte, I was upset about it. I experienced the same type of trauma, I am sure.

When I was in college, we played in the Sugar Bowl Basketball Tournament in New Orleans. That was the first time I had ever seen separate black and white restrooms and drinking fountains. In Charlotte, I experienced the same thing. How do you explain something like that to a man like Coop? I didn't have the sophistication at that time to deal with it. I didn't know what to say to the guy. I searched for the appropriate thing to say, but couldn't find it. Rather than say something stupid, I didn't say anything at all.

By the time Russell arrived six years later, there were more black players in the league but still not very many. I'm sure there were a lot of subtle incidents that happened to him. But as far as team incidents go, there were very few, if any. Russ was aloof from the start. Completely. Russell never responded to hecklers because he knew recognizing them was the wrong approach. He didn't want them to know they had gotten his attention. He did not give them satisfaction. He's always carried himself this way.

In a sense, all jocks, black or white, do this. It is a form of security not to let the outside world know what we are really like. Russ is still that way. But in the locker room, he was a different guy. He was outgoing. He was witty. He was clever. He was talking constantly. It was as if he'd been in a shell all day dealing with the outside world, but in a comfortable environment he could shed that shell and be himself. I am sure Russ prefers to be outgoing, that is his natural self. The shell is a defense mechanism.

Playing golf with Bill Russell can be a very pleasurable experience. From the first hole to the last he laughs and jokes. He is fun to be with. He is excellent company in this environment. Yet he can be an embarrassment outside of it.

Auerbach knew from the start that Russell would be treated differently than the average rookie. Arnold always knew when to use the big stick and when not to, and with Russell it was definitely a "not to." Russell was going to be our saviour, and, as a result, he did not go through the normal rookie indoctrination (History Repeating Itself Dept.: Twenty-eight years later Michael Jordan was accorded the same instant hero status by the Bulls). Russell didn't carry the bags, get the Cokes, get stuck paying the cabbie, or any of the other things all Celtic rookies used to do. Poor John Havlicek went through the indoctrination for *two* years because no rookie was able to make the club his second season. Russ didn't go through it for five minutes or five seconds.

Under Auerbach, there was always a designated whipping boy. Most of the time it was supposed to be a good-natured thing. Russell got kidded but not hazed. As time went on, he and I got special treatment in the sense that Arnold only got on those he thought he could get on. Russ and I came with so much intensity that getting on us would have been counterproductive. It wouldn't have made any sense to get me pissed off for any reason, and the same certainly applied to Russ.

Auerbach kept order and sanity for himself in his own way. There would be a practical joke—very big in those days—and Arnold would get pissed off. All of a sudden there would be a meeting and he would scream and cuss for ten or fifteen minutes. He would aim his anger at us but never directly at any one person. He would make it general. It would be, "You guys." We'd know who Red meant. The point is that he would get it out of his system. I don't know how the other guys felt.

People always ask me about how Frank Ramsey dealt with race. He was from Kentucky and was even nicknamed the "Kentucky Colonel." People often assume Ramsey had a problem playing with black players, but he certainly did not.

Ramsey was a bright and classy guy who was also very expedient. I have no idea how he feels in his heart, but I doubt he was that good an actor. Predictably, Rams became a multimillionaire. He had himself completely under control. He was much more mature than the rest of us.

I played seven years with Russ and I honestly didn't think we had a personal problem. Long after we retired, I read and heard that Russell supposedly felt slighted because the press made me the focus of the game accounts, rather than him. This is going to sound naive, but I really wasn't aware of that. I was insensitive to it because I didn't care. Even if I had acknowledged it, what could I have done about it? I thought I was handling situations as well as I possibly could. Looking back, maybe I wasn't taking proper advantage of my role.

At the time, the press in Boston was all white, of course, and in general not very knowledgeable about basketball. I had always been their boy, going back to my Holy Cross days. But they had to realize how good Russell was. Maybe the problem wasn't local but national. Was he getting his share of the national attention early enough? Maybe not. But should that have any bearing on what has gone on since? In retirement, who has been credited with being the foundation of the Celtics' dynasty? Bill Russell. He's gotten his due from all of us. That doesn't mean he wasn't uncomfortable back then.

The implication is that the white media favored the white guy at the expense of the black guy. In Russell's eyes, this is an example of Boston's racism. It could very well have happened, and I was insensitive to it. Who knows? You're surrounded by the media and you're talking to people. You don't notice who else they're talking to.

But thinking back, none of this came out. It didn't interfere with our personal relationship. We had a normal teammate relationship. We didn't socialize together that much and we were never really close. We were compatible teammates. But those were different times. Without articulating it, I knew, for example, that I couldn't invite Russ to the Worcester Country Club to play golf.

The entire relationship is different in college than it is in the pros. In college, you're more sensitive to everything. As a pro, you come to practice and to games—especially when you live in Worcester, as I did—and then you go on your way.

Russ just came in and established not only that he had a personality, but that he would *be* a personality.

Russell came in cleanshaven. Then he grew a goatee. That was kind of radical in those days, something you associated with jazz musicians, perhaps, and not many other people. One year, he started wearing a cape. This tends to get your attention. This wasn't like K.C. Jones coming in and us not being sure of the sound of his voice for about two years because he was so quiet. Russell made an immediate impact. Russ established his identity when he arrived, and he continued to add on to and get more set in his ways as he made whatever point it was he wished to make. This may have been a means, even then, of divorcing himself from a world he thought was hostile. Or Russell may just have been moody. But all of it was his face to the outside world.

It was obvious from the start of Russell's career, both in terms of Auerbach's setting the lead and my leadership as captain, that there was never going to be a bad apple on our team. There was only going to be a positive atmosphere. It was clear to anyone coming in that if they weren't in tune with the racial attitude of our ball club, they weren't going to be tolerated. We couldn't govern what the fans were thinking and saying, unfortunately, but in our unit it was so obvious that even the most redneck southerner, had one come in, would have been overwhelmed.

I think the fact that blacks came in so slowly helped the so-called integration situation. Race is more of an issue now, and it's a different issue. Now whites are the minority, and I don't think it makes a helluva lot of difference to the players involved. A teammate is a teammate.

People are people and Bill Russell, Sam Jones, K.C. Jones, and Satch Sanders are all different personalities. As I've said, I believe racism is rooted in insecurity. I'd say that Sam, K.C., and Satch approached the problem from a purely pragmatic standpoint. That's the way most of us would. I'm sure it's the way I would. We compromise where necessary in our self-interest.

In that sense Russ—and here is where I admire Russ—was proud enough and secure enough to ignore them all. He thumbed his nose at anyone he wanted to, and he's still doing it, because he's a strong enough person not to compromise his principles. While he was playing, and therefore dealing from a perceived power base, the haters were all saying, "Some day that son of a bitch will get his." He hasn't yet. I admire that quality. I wish I were that strong. I walk kind of a middle line. It's the old cliché: How much the individual will compromise depends on what's at stake. We all give ourselves the benefit of the doubt.

I would like to think that I will never compromise past a certain point in terms of integrity. Russ never even made that concession. He has *never* compromised. Of the other three, Sam probably feels the strongest about this. I have seen enough of Sam in action in terms of public relations and the things he does that he will do what he has to do. He goes to functions that you know he isn't pleased to be at. I hate to go to some of those things myself. I go out of my way for Nabisco, for example, and I think I do a hell of a job. Team RJR

Nabisco is the premier sports marketing vehicle in this country. It allows older jocks with good credibility in the marketplace to stay active. I'm not saying I hate it, necessarily, but if I didn't have to do it, I probably wouldn't.

Russ doesn't. I suppose now that he's no longer coaching in Sacramento people are saying, "What the hell is he doing now? He's taking all that money. Or what did he ever do in Seattle?" The answer is that he did what he wanted to do, and he did it on his terms. He is *still* doing it on his terms.

The only time Russ has come out of his shell is for expedient reasons. He is the last person in the world who would ever participate in an Old Timers' Game for reasons of pragmatism and pride. I felt the same way for many years, but relented when it became a matter of serving a good cause (a foundation for old-timers in need). I also realized I probably wouldn't do myself any harm. So in my own mind it wasn't that big a deal.

Russ is still motivated by pride and the fact that now he doesn't want to give all those haters he assumes are out there—unfortunately, he may be right—the opportunity to see him at anything less than his best. Maybe if I were him I'd do the same thing. Crawl back in my shell and don't expose myself to any weakness, in this case a deteriorating body and game. My hostilities, for what they were worth, wouldn't parallel how strongly and deeply Russell feels.

I don't know how much of Russ's feelings are the product of paranoia or of justifiable rage due to racism. If I were black, I think I'd be a bomb thrower. I'd certainly be a marcher. I don't know that I would have acted a lot differently than Bill Russell has acted. But it takes a very strong and secure person to do that. I think this is what Russell has demonstrated. Most people just make do and live with the situation. That is not Bill Russell's way.

— 5 —

Russ vs. Wilt

WHAT FUN IS it to discuss Bill Russell without mentioning his rivalry with Wilt Chamberlain? Yes, basketball is a team game, but within that context, Russell and Chamberlain were the most celebrated individual rivalry in the history of the sport.

More fuel was dumped on the fire in the fall of 1987 when Harvey Pollack, a 76ers executive who was the public relations man for both the old Philly Warriors and the 76ers for most of the past 42 years, issued the definitive statistical comparison of the rivalry in his 76ers press guide. Harvey's numbers revealed that Chamberlain outscored and outrebounded Russell. According to Harvey, that settles it. Chamberlain was a better player than Russell.

Harvey is wrong.

Russell had much more intensity than Wilt and skills better suited to playing basketball. Russell made us all better players. Wilt, in my opinion, had the opposite effect on teams.

Wilt was such an individualistic player that, rather

than help his teammates, he would often generate petty jealousies. Teammates were told to wait until Wilt came downcourt, to get it inside to Wilt, etc., rather than look for their own scoring opportunities. There was resentment on the part of other players who thought they shot better than Wilt, or who had talents that weren't being exploited. It was just the opposite with Russell because he took care of himself only after helping us out. We didn't have to take care of him.

There's a postscript to this. The question has often been asked, "What would have happened to the Celtics if Wilt had played for them instead of Russell?" First, it's never clear if Russell is to be factored into this equation by playing for another team against the Celtics. Let's say he isn't. We can assume the Celtics would have won *something* with Wilt. If Wilt had been surrounded by our talent, he would have won some championships. Whether that number would have been three, four, five, or six is anyone's guess. But it definitely would not have been eleven of thirteen.

I know it's difficult for some people to comprehend how you can say a guy who was capable of scoring 50 points a game for an entire season, and 100 points in a single game, isn't better than Bill Russell, who never scored 40 points in an NBA game.

You've got to understand the game. The chemistry we had with Russell as a running team would not have been there with Chamberlain. I would not have waited for Wilt to get set up so we could pass him the ball. I wouldn't have cared if he could score 100 points in every game.

Maybe you had to see Wilt and Russ play against each other to understand the difference. The fact is that Wilt was bigger (7′1″ vs. 6′9″) and stronger (275 pounds or so vs. 225 pounds), and could take it to the basket at will—except against us. Russell intimidated him. Wilt can say what he wants, but I used to watch Wilt muscle in against everyone else, but not against Russell. He would never do that. That's how his fadeaway jump shot was born. Russell forced Wilt to develop that shot.

In our games, Russ's strategy was simple: Force Wilt just a little bit on the sides so he couldn't muscle it in with a spin move, using one dribble or no dribbles. If Wilt got Russ under the basket he could, in fact, overpower him.

Wilt wanted to take it to the middle, but he wasn't good enough handling the basketball to do it against us. He kind of took little steps, and he'd have to dribble it two or three times. By then, the ball was gone. If Russ didn't have it, one of us did, and we were running down the court in the other direction.

The psychology between them was fascinating. Russ would dig in from the start. He didn't have to be told the importance of this rivalry. Wilt would get his offensive rebounds and his power stuff, and once in a while make an individual move, but Russ wouldn't let him sustain it. He might even do it for a game, but maybe he would do it with the fadeaway, but there was no way he would beat Russell over a period of time using the fadeaway as his basic weapon.

Wilt was a paradox. Because he was so effective, coaches wanted him to score 40 points a game or more. But he still had to play with four other people. Wilt was a complete individualist, but you can't use that as an excuse. I really don't think Wilt ever understood that basketball is a team sport and unless all five players participate, you would not win. One year, Wilt averaged 50 points a game. By the end of his career all he did was pass. He never seemed to catch on.

Basketball is a true team sport. The success of the whole is predicated on all five people reacting to one another, as opposed to one guy hitting eighty-eight home runs and the others tagging along. Wilt's incessant search for individual records, whether it was scoring, rebounding, or assists, indicates to me he never really understood how the game should be played to win those championships he always talked about.

That brings us to the fact that Russell was the catalyst for our teams. He molded the team and made the talents blend. We had our share of letdowns and mood swings, although probably not as many as teams have today. One reason we had fewer than anyone, I am sure, was the nature of Bill Russell's game. I suspect it caused us to overachieve more than the Philadelphia players.

None of this may make sense to Wilt. He has the numbers. Russell will always have the rings. It was no accident.

— 6 —

Motivation

I COULD WATCH the NBA playoffs endlessly. I don't care who's playing. I am so competitive that whenever people are trying to accomplish a goal, and giving 100 percent to do it, it turns me on. If it's basketball, the only time I know I'm going to get that consistency of effort is during the playoffs.

For the same reason, if I never have to go to another exhibition game, in any sport, basketball included, I will be very happy. During the season, unfortunately, I think it's safe to say there are inconsistencies in effort today—certainly more than there were in the fifties and sixties. The truth is that it's harder to motivate people today, and the problem starts long before a player ever reaches the professional level.

It's tough being a coach, at any time in history, and it's toughest of all right now. Think of the Billy Martin self-destructions. Throw in Hubie Brown and Bill Fitch. You are not dealing with machines. You are dealing with human beings. The problem is much more serious today, in terms of egos because good young players are spoiled from the time they are in grammar school. This did not happen with us. We didn't sign big contracts. We were not hounded by 200 college recruiters, so there were fewer forces at work. We came to play.

The NBA schedule has always been demanding. We averaged four games a week. I don't know what it is today, but the point is that you have to be a damn machine to function at peak efficiency. Some fan will come up to me and ask, "How can they beat that team by twenty one night and lose by twenty two nights later?" They say it's fixed, and all that.

Fans can't relate to what's going on. They don't understand there is some son of a bitch across the blue line who is earning less money than you, and who has less talent, but on this occasion he is more motivated than you are because it *is* you.

To be consistent, you must come to the fray with the same emotional high every game. This is impossible to do. This is why a team like the Celtics goes on the road and plays with such tremendous inconsistency. They'll come out and play well one night and then come out flat against a team like the Clippers, playing three awful quarters and finding themselves behind before pulling it out in the fourth quarter with a little burst of effort. It's because athletes are the most pragmatic of animals. Given half a chance, they will always select the path of least resistance.

If they know they can come out and beat the Clippers by playing a quarter of basketball, that is what they will try to do. This can backfire, and that's why there are more upsets today. That's why I think there are fewer upsets in the basketball playoffs than in any other sport.

This lassitude is especially true if the superior team is on the road. At home, there may be positive forces at work. But on the road, if you can get it done in a period, you'll try to do just that. At home, you may be inclined to play hard for at least the first two periods, to put away the other team. After that, a good team can loaf at home and get away with it. The Celtics have had fabulous success in the Boston Garden for the past three years, especially. But, yes, they do let down a lot there. This mode of thinking really started catching up with them last year.

With the offensive weapons the Celtics have, they can let down at home and still blow a team away, or be successful on the road by picking their spots, and, obviously, for the last two years they have been getting away with it—to a point.

But cracks have begun to show the past year or so —they lost two playoff games in the Garden to Detroit in one series—and they may have to reevaluate their approach. They'll have to create a new mindset. That will be one of Jimmy Rodgers's major tasks as he succeeds K.C. Jones as coach.

Player motivation will be tough, for him, or for anybody. As we continue to create more spoiled, self-centered, and highly paid athletes, the inconsistencies in terms of blocking and tackling in football, or defensive rebounding in basketball—the so-called "dirty jobs"—will become greater, and you'll have more upsets during the season. I don't believe there will ever be another dynasty in sports for those reasons. Give credit to Pat Riley and the Lakers for defending their championship last season. I didn't believe they could do it. They have succeeded against the monster we have created in sports, one that is born in high school and is nurtured in college.

Fans translate everything into dollar signs. If a player is paid X amount of dollars, he must perform to that level every night. That's the ideal, but it doesn't work that way in practice. You're still talking about a human being—who may be having an off night. In the case of Larry Bird, whose effort can never be questioned, he had an off series against Detroit last season. In general terms, the money isn't going to change a guy's nature. It doesn't work that way, no matter what you pay him. With ticket prices escalating (as a result of increasing player salaries, in the fan's view), fans are becoming more and more agitated. They are paying more for tickets. They are far less patient, and far more fickle.

So who can handle these players? What qualities are necessary to be a successful coach in this league?

I think the requisite in professional basketball is your intensity, your concern about winning and losing. If I were hiring a coach, the first quality I would seek would be the ability to motivate. That would supersede everything. Over the long term motivation is more meaningful in player–coach relationships and in getting players to sustain their efforts a little longer than the next fellow. In college, it's different. Most coaches can motivate college players, but it's usually not that big an issue because it happens almost automatically. Unless a coach has communication problems, his kids generally come in sky-high or simply need a little goose. You're talking about thirty games over a span of four or five months. As a rule, players in college supply their own motivation. Coaches don't have to bring it out. When you get to the pro level for an eight-month season, coaches need to understand human nature. It's not just an intellectual understanding of it, either. It must be, in my opinion, a reflection of your personality, which means you've got to be demonstrative. You've got to smack lockers, if that's what it takes, and you've got to continue to do it. Despite the sophistication of the jock and the Frankenstein's monster we've created, I still think the best way to reach the jock and establish a rapport is genuine sincerity. It's all got to be a reflection of your personality, as they know you.

If you're going to smack a locker and have tears running down your face, it's only going to have an impact if they know that's *you*. If they know it's not you, your behavior will have no effect at all. They will laugh you out of the place. You must give them genuine sustained proof of how *badly* you want it and how much you're willing to sacrifice to achieve it.

Sometimes drastic measures are necessary, even in college. I had a situation when I was coaching at Boston College where I got a little dramatic. We were playing in the 1966 Sugar Bowl Tournament in New Orleans. It was an excellent Christmas tournament. Utah, Tennessee, and our team all were ranked in the Top Twenty. Bradley, which won the tournament, had an excellent club. We lost the first game to Utah by two, and I was worried because we had to play a very good Tennessee team the next night in the third place game. We needed that game to maintain our ranking, and consolation games are notoriously treacherous, even in a situation like that. The disappointment of losing the first game is often hard to overcome when there is no longer a chance of winning the tournament. The tendency is to let down, where winning the first game sustains the emotion.

I know that teams can let down. We were a long way from home, and Tennessee was a quality opponent. I went through all kinds of emotional hell prior to that game, including a crazy tantrum that ended with me smashing my fist into the blackboard.

One of my players, center Willie Wolters, came up to me after that performance and said, "Jesus, coach. Why didn't you tell us? We didn't know you wanted the game *that* bad." The point is, they got the message. But if you tried to do that every game, you'd be in a strait-jacket by midseason. You can't put your system on emotional highs and lows that often.

Realistically, in the pros the coach is the only one who suffers to that degree. Today, I watch the players after a bad loss, and they're just screwing around as if they don't care. In that sense, I still respond like an old-timer. I know you can't turn off the rock music in the locker room, and you can't have players sit on their hands in somber fashion when they get on the bus after a tough loss. But you'd like to see *some* reaction. The problem is, they can rationalize, "Well, what the hell. It's not important. What happens in April is important." They don't understand that it's not a faucet deal. If you don't have all the groundwork laid before you get to the playoffs, you're not going to be able to turn it on when you get there.

The Celtics last year really needed motivation. They have been drifting away from a passionate commitment to winning for two years. They believe they can turn it on and turn it off. Night after night, I've weatched them do good things offensively and get a ten-point lead late in the first quarter or early in the second, but I know they're heading for trouble because the sustained defensive commitment isn't there. So I'll say on the air that it's going to be a close game, and it generally turns out that way. If it's a road game, it probably turns into a loss.

Players don't believe this happens. The truth is, we didn't, either, thirty years ago. I used to talk about it with K.C. Jones. We always thought we had the capacity to turn it on and turn it off. We picked our spots, just like these guys do. We'd go into Madison Square Garden—I can't emphasize how important a venue that was in those days—and we'd want to do our thing offensively. It's always easy to summon the energy to play offense.

When players always say, "I tried as hard as I could," they normally are referring to offense. But they aren't as interested in meeting their man at halfcourt, digging in, or in any way trapping with the same alertness they do when they're down by two with a couple of minutes to go.

Auerbach would come into the huddle I don't know how many times after he watched this stuff take place and launch a tirade. This usually took place on the road because at home we were usually twenty points up. He'd use a few well-chosen obscenities. "Fucking guys. We are stuck here. Do you mind working for at least eight minutes tonight? Russ, would you go out and play that fucking dummy? Would you stop letting that guy shoot? He's hit four outside shots in a row, so would you mind playing him for a while? You know he can't put it on the floor."

That would be it. We'd go back out, and—boom— the game would soon be over. We had the capacity to change. I can't believe we had a more competitive spirit. I simply believe disintegrating forces have been at work on teams since then. That was about the only time Arnold ever used to give us pep talks, when he wanted to seize the momentum. I don't know if it worked *every* time, but I recall that it worked many, many times. I think our accomplishments were greater because in those years there were fewer teams and the talent was more concentrated. You didn't have the talent differential that has existed for most of the eighties between the Lakers and Celtics and most of their opponents. But we used to come out of those huddles and literally raise it up another notch. Today's players may think they can control their destiny, but when it comes time, they very often can't.

*   *   *

A coach must always worry about his team's emotional state. As difficult as it may be to believe, a team can even be vulnerable to a letdown during the playoffs. The game I used to worry most about was the first game at home in a five- or seven-game series. Say you just came through one emotional series, and you've had a bitch of a time. This year the Celtics played a seventh game against Atlanta that was a great struggle. Bird scored twenty points in the fourth quarter, and they pulled it out. Detroit came in and beat the Celtics in the first game of the next series. Emotion is more of a problem for the home team than the road team in the playoffs, if both teams are coming out of tough series. It's the first game the home team has the best chance of losing because it's easier for the road team to bring itself out of it than the home team. The combination of the emotional high you are coming down from, and the comfortable feeling of being at home may cause you to relax. You think you can relax a little, and get away with it. The result of all this is a flat game, in which the home team, even if it is the superior club, can lose. During the season it doesn't work this way because the visiting team does not come in with a sustained effort, and so a mediocre performance at home will get the job done.

Teams are also emotionally vulnerable after they've played one of the NBA's elite during the regular season. Teams get up so high to play the Lakers or the Celtics that you're fortunate to catch them the next night.

What's intriguing about the current Celtics and their attitude is that there aren't any bad-asses on the club. You would think a coach would be able to reach them.

But there is a pervasive attitude on this team about what is and what isn't important that has the potential to come back to haunt them.

There was an ongoing situation last season with Danny Ainge and three-pointers. He became infatuated with the shot. True, the three-point shot is a useful weapon when used properly, and Ainge can point to some tremendously direct benefits. There were at least two games in which his three-pointers in the second half won games for the Celtics they would otherwise have lost. He hit six against New York in a double over-time win in November and he hit six in a nice win over Utah. And there were many other times the shot helped the ball club.

But there were, in my judgment, many other times Ainge's three-pointers hurt the team, and I never tired of pointing this out during our broadcasts. One problem was that he had the official green light from K.C. Jones, who reasoned that to put any kind of restriction on Ainge would be to risk losing the benefits of the skill.

I once talked to K.C. about it. He assured me that Danny was a good kid who didn't in any way want to be destructive, that Danny was a gung-ho player who really wanted to win, and that he, K.C., didn't want to impede the kid.

I don't think Ainge knew when to pull the trigger and when not to. I just don't think that was the way to go in the long run, and I think I was vindicated by his performance in the playoffs. Opponents concentrated a lot more on stopping the three-pointer during the playoffs, and it seemed to disrupt Ainge's entire offensive game. He shot under forty percent for the playoffs. Those three- or four-foot sliding putts you make so easily in a Wednesday golf match become absolutely terrifying and almost impossible to drop when it's tournament time.

The reason I get so upset about Ainge's three-point obsession is that he is in no way exploiting his vast talent by making the long-range shot such a focal point of his game. Danny rationalizes that he can make that shot forty percent of the time, which is the equivalent of fifty percent two-point shooting, and so that's that. He ignores the impact the shot has on anything else the team wants to do in the halfcourt. He ignores the fact that this team's strength is inside. Most importantly, he ignores the fact that with his quickness and ball-handling ability, he can always create a better opportunity for himself, which is what I used to tell Tiny Archibald. "In your entire career," I would tell him, "you should never take a bad shot. There is no reason to. You can always create something better for yourself than what you think you have." To some degree, Danny Ainge is in the same position.

When you have the three-pointer in your blood, you have a tendency to take them at the wrong time. Even Bird does that on occasion, although he has made more intelligent use of the three-pointer than anyone in the history of the rule. An occasional bad shot comes with the territory. But Danny doesn't have Larry's overall good sense with the shot.

The three-pointer can be a trap, with psychological effects for both teams. It makes offensive life too easy in the short run and reduces the will to work at the fundamentals of offense. A player has to be motivated to exercise the requisite discipline with the shot.

Has the damage been done to the Celtics? The Celtics were at their best in the 1985–86 season, when the only person cranking up the threes was Bird. Last year's team needed a little extra boost in the beginning of the season because Kevin McHale was out of the lineup recuperating from foot surgery. He was forced to miss the first fourteen games of the season. Maybe it made sense for the Celtics to depend on Ainge's three-pointers as a consistent source of offense. That was one way to win. But eventually McHale came back and it was necessary to find a new balance.

Ainge has a different self-image than he did two years ago. He's made the All-Star Team, and the primary focus was those three-point shots. If you're Danny Ainge, you've got to fight this. Can he learn to properly complement his tremendous physical talent, or has he allowed the success of last season override his good common sense in terms of what's good for the team?

I don't think Danny Ainge is in any way a selfish player. He *will* make the pass. It's a very subtle thing: he now believes that because he can shoot the three-pointer so effectively he should take it whenever he can, rather than exercising his options and getting into whatever halfcourt play the team is supposed to be running. Don't "search it out." It will always be there. Most of the time, the Celtics want to go inside. If that doesn't materialize, then they get it out and Ainge may wind up taking that shot as a last resort. If he continually takes it as a first option, he takes it without recognizing the destructive potential it has.

A team as experienced and intelligent as the Celtics should be concerned with one thing offensively—searching out the best shot. A coach has to focus on exactly what it is that makes these guys so effective. For the past eight or nine years the Celtics have been successful, first, because they continually look inside first and, second, because they search out the best shot. Bird sometimes makes implementing this philosophy difficult because he can disrupt everything. Bird can do things wrong and have it come out right.

Dennis Johnson got back to doing something he does very well last year, which is taking it to the basket. Bird has observed that he knows when DJ is really ready to play when he's taking it to the basket. If Johnson does that, he can create things just about every time. It means hard work for him, and Johnson knows that in going inside he's likely to get clobbered. That's fine, DJ is so strong that he can overpower even bigger players.

A basic problem for all coaches in this league is the fact that most players think they are better shooters than they are. You try to instill the idea of searching out the best possible shot each time down the floor, but players exercise questionable judgments of what is and what isn't a good shot for them.

I remain a big believer that a team's basic offense must start from the inside and work outward, rather than vice versa. As soon as I look at a stat sheet, and I see a team getting a disproportionate amount of its scoring from the backcourt, I see trouble. Any time you've got a guard-oriented offense on the NBA level, you are definitely in trouble. You can't win consistently having your guards as the high scorers. If they are, it either means that they happen to be your best offensive talents or that they have not done a good enough job searching out the best shots for the ball club.

Getting a point like this through to players—or any other point for that matter—is often not easy. The Celtics went through a long period in which they automatically did things the right way offensively, but over the past two seasons they have begun to drift away. They got away from what was proper, for whatever reason. Was it because K.C. Jones was so incredibly passive? I don't know. It's easy to blame K.C., and I've got to qualify that criticism with the fact that the coach on this level often has so little impact on players, not only in terms of what happens on the court on a nightly basis, but also in terms of affecting the minds of the players.

I've been a part of this league for 38 years, and I

don't remember the last time I heard a player, in social conversation or otherwise, give the coach credit. We didn't do it when we played, and there's even less chance of hearing it now. Our spoiled athletes have all the answers and figure they must be great players because their contracts and their agents tell them so. Once they sign that big contract, they think they know it all, and it's much more difficult for the coach to reach them and change their minds.

It's harder today for a coach to seize and maintain control. Sometimes losing can be beneficial in the short term if it gets the players' attention and allows you to reinforce your coaching theories. Tell them something, and if it works you've made your point. On this level, if whatever you tell them doesn't work quickly, however, they start to raise questions, and your authority starts to evaporate.

If it's difficult to motivate a team that has talent, and knows that if they put forth the requisite effort they can accomplish great things, then can you conceive of how difficult it must be to motivate a team with meager talent, a team that knows that its best effort will not come close to defeating a good team playing with minimal inspiration. Can you imagine, what it was like to be Gene Shue with the 1987–88 Los Angeles Clippers?

The Clippers didn't start off badly last year. They played low-scoring, ball-control games and they benefitted from a schedule that placed them at home quite a bit during the months of November and December. As the season hit the 25-game mark, Shue became apprehensive. He wondered what would happen when the club hit the road and when the identity of its home foes grew tougher. The Clippers collapsed. By New Year's Day they were once again the worst team in the league.

As good a coach and communicator as a man may be, he can only make players believe up to a point. In college, you might make players believe throughout the season, and they continue to give the best effort for twenty-five college games, even though they wind up 5–20. At that level you can maintain their enthusiasm if you work at it.

In the case of a Gene Shue, thank goodness he won four or five games early to use as bait to keep the Clippers in there for the first quarter of the season. But once they had a protracted stretch on the road, and started getting blown out, despite their enthusiasm, they started to deteriorate. If you get destroyed early, the rest of the road trip can be a disaster.

It's even worse if you're trying to get something from an in-and-outer such as Benoit Benjamin. A guy like that will really give you an ulcer. He can shoot and he can block shots, and he has really caused the Celtics, among many others, problems inside. But when Benjamin is going good, it's just one phase of the moon. Benoit can respond to the challenge of the better players, but unfortunately he lets down against the weaker centers.

When things are going bad it's so easy to give in to all the problems. The way to develop consistency is to work hard at the least attractive elements of the game, things like defense. Conversely, it is far easier to turn your mind off to those departments and concentrate on putting up a few shots that might give you good personal numbers at contract time.

The better teams know they've got the talent, and that when they apply themselves good things should happen. The weaker teams know they're the weaker teams, and that when they shy away from a 100 percent effort in such areas as rebounding, the situation can explode in their faces. The sad reality is that it's easier for the weak teams to turn away from the dirty jobs than it is for the better teams, who know they can still blow you away with offense. It's easier to play offense than defense, so the weaker teams are at a disadvantage psychologically. It's a nightmare. That's why a guy like Rick Pitino, who comes charging out of college, where he had players practicing at 7:00 in the morning and believing they could do just about anything—as getting to the Final Four demonstrated—has to be frustrated with the reality of professional life. At some point, Pitino realizes he is not going to get through to some people.

Atmosphere can be vital. It's nice coming to play in the Boston Garden or the Forum or any continually sold out arena where there is legitimate excitement each and every night. For the Clippers, it has been as if they were the JV team to the Lakers' varsity. Even when there are fans in the stands, they are apathetic. What a base for forty-one games, to feel that you're in the backwash of the league.

Or take a recent loser—the New Jersey Nets. It's a godforsaken situation. The building the Nets play in is nice enough, but you don't even feel you are in the NBA when you take the floor. The fans sit on their hands even when the building is sold out. For some reason, they still haven't developed a relationship with the team they're supposed to be rooting and cheering for. The Nets need every home court advantage they can muster. They're not getting it.

Graphic illustration of the value of motivation was provided for us all last year by Doug Moe, who so over-inspired his team he wound up being named Coach of the Year.

No one has ever accused Doug Moe of being a master tactician. He would gag if anyone did. He is the original laid-back guy. He has always kept his practices short and his theories simple. He wins a lot more than he loses. He never has two bad years in a row. He's got a style that is very difficult to prepare for in the short run. Perhaps people should start paying more attention to him.

Last year's Denver Nuggets team was an amazing outfit. On paper, that team simply didn't compare with many of the top clubs. Moe obviously motivates his players. His teams work hard to create turnovers on defense and they move the ball well on offense.

Moe can do things with odd-sized players, or guys with unique skills that no one else can use. For years, he has derived great mileage from T.R. Dunn, a 6'4" guard who can't shoot but can get to the offensive boards. Dunn hustles continually. He also has a strange professional love-hate relationship with Bill Hanzlik, a 6'7" guy who didn't even average ten points a game in college (Notre Dame). Hanzlik is a kamikaze type who gets after you on defense. He has been able to guard everyone from point guards to Ralph Sampson. Incidentally, both Hanzlik and Dunn were obtained in trades, which means they were obtained for a purpose.

Moe's big reclamation project last season was Michael Adams, a guard who had been released two years earlier by Sacramento. Adams was a throw-in when the Nuggets obtained Jay Vincent from the Washington Bullets for Darrell Walker and Mark Alarie. Adams had never really done much for Washington, although Magic Johnson did observe during the 1988 playoffs that Adams had once "beaten us all by himself" while performing for the Bullets.

On most teams, Adams would have been more of a nuisance than an asset. He is a total helter-skelter player. He dribbles excessively, and you can never be sure where he's going on the court, at either end. Most coaches would view Adams as disruptive, but he turned out to be ideal for Moe.

Doug creates a kind of laissez-faire atmosphere where his players never feel inhibited. His basic offense is the so-called "passing game," a pass-and-pick-away style that features constant offensive movement. There are certain principles, but it all comes down to getting the right feel for what's going on. Not every player is suited to it.

There are years when Moe's teams really don't plug themselves into the passing game. Last year was not one of those seasons. In fact, it may very well be that no previous Moe team, be it in the ABA or the NBA, has ever more thoroughly bought the offensive philosophy. One of the key elements was Adams. He seemed to tie everything together.

This, to me, is what coaching at the NBA level is really all about. Moe did with Michael Adams what I wanted to do with Tiny Archibald. Here was a kid hardly removed from the Continental Basketball Association, but Moe saw something in him and gave him tremendous responsibility. The kid relates to it. He is obviously playing over his head, but Moe understands human nature. He's turning to an underdog, giving him responsibility, and demonstrating tremendous faith in the kid.

This approach can be applied to any team that acquires a new player. A player joins the team anxious to prove what he can do. He will overachieve because he overworks. The coach who understands that gives Michael Adams an opportunity. Next year, Michael Adams may go back where he belongs, so to speak.

Even Jay Vincent was noticeably more efficient last season, in between injuries. Here is a 6'7" guy whose forte is offense. He had his problems in Dallas and they shipped him to Washington. I think we can safely say he flopped in Washington. When he got to Denver, Doug Moe told him, "You're my man," and he started to achieve.

They used to call that TV producer Freddy Silverman "The Man with the Golden Gut" in deference to his amazing instinct for hit shows as he sifted through the tons of pilots each season. I'd have to call Doug Moe the NBA's "Man with the Golden Gut," because I don't think any other coach reads the emotional state of his team the way he does.

In 1987 the Celtics arrived in Denver for a game. Moe told everyone who would listen that the Nuggets had no shot at winning the game. "Take the points," he kidded before the game, "and take *extra* points." The Celtics annihilated the Nuggets.

This past season we arrived in Denver. The Celtics had won a nice game in Phoenix, but Moe was unimpressed. "I not only think we're going to win," he said before the game, "but I think we're gonna blow you people out." I don't know too many coaches in this league who would talk like that.

And I'm sure he took full advantage of the situation. He probably got in there before the game and said, "Forget all that bullshit about the big, bad Celtics. I've got confidence in you. I know damned good and well you can kick their asses if you bring it to them." You send a team out there like that and a lot of positive things can happen. Moe understands that. So what if he's not a big X and O guy? At this level that's not a priority.

The passing game gets the job done. The biggest knock on it has always been that when things get sticky in the closing minutes of a tight game, it doesn't necessarily get the ball to the top scorers where they can do the most damage. Critics say too often the wrong guy winds up taking the wrong shot. This is, of course, irrelevant if you're up by twenty with two minutes to go, which the Nuggets often were last year. That team is no fun to play. Kevin McHale said last year that they're the only team in the league that can make seven or eight passes and still have eight seconds left on the twenty-four-second clock. He said that we'll make three or four and be done, and other teams will make four and the clock is ready to go off. The Nuggets last year absolutely believed in what they were doing, and it showed.

Moe has survived a long time, and his demeanor has never changed. He doesn't look much worse for wear, either. He doesn't kill himself. He doesn't make coaching a twenty-four-hour obsession. He enjoys himself away from the court. But watch him work the sidelines when the game starts. This man is really into the game. He's very competitive. Despite his self-deprecating remarks and his wisecracks, Moe is no clown. He wants to win as much as anybody. He gets on the officials. He has, in fact, probably paid as much money in fines for things he's said about officials than anyone in the game. You always know he's around.

And let's put one thing to rest right now. The Nuggets have the image of the ultimate run-and-gun team, but what's always triggered their offense is their excellent pressure defense. They really aren't blessed with a bunch of great shooters. They must put the ball up ten or fifteen times more than their opponents each night, and they've got to get to the foul line more often if they are to be successful. Defense is what turned them into a great team last year. Nobody gets more easy baskets than they do, and that's a tribute to their defense.

Getting to people is the key. I mentioned Benoit Benjamin before because he seems to be the ultimate modern-day example of a kid loaded with talent who can't quite get the drift of the whole thing. If he's not over-eating, he's standing at the top of the key firing up jump shots, instead of getting underneath where he can do the most damage. Something has to be done about him.

But what? You can't change a kid's personality. The Kings have tried. They brought in Willis Reed, who recruited him from Louisiana to Creighton, to tutor him. They even brought in Bill Russell to tutor him. Benjamin doesn't appear to be any closer to getting in the All-Star Game than he ever was. Meanwhile, he probably wonders what the fussing and fuming is all about. He's being paid about a million dollars a year to put his coach, general manager, and owner into early graves.

I have a theory that it may be easier to get to a kid like Benjamin in a small city. I think that environment has accounted for some of Don Nelson's success over the years in Milwaukee. John MacLoed, when he was in Phoenix, may fall into this category, as well. As a general rule I'd say you have a better chance to be a motivator in Denver and Milwaukee than in, say, Los Angeles or New York. You have better access to the players's psyches in a small town atmosphere.

It seems to me that while all of today's players yearn to be macho and sophisticated, they don't all have the same opportunity to express themselves. They might have to cling to the unit more in a small city than they will in a larger market, where they just show up for practices and games and then go their own way.

The coach has got to know who he is. He's got to have a way of dealing with pressure. Jack Ramsay is a nice example. He's intense, yes, and prepared, yes, and disciplined, yes, and structured, yes. He's been around for twenty years, and he's learned how to keep his sanity and his composure.

I was talking with Jim Paxson shortly after he joined the Celtics about Dr. Jack, who had been Paxson's coach in Portland for several years. He explained that Ramsay's release was exercise. Jack is sixty-three years old and in phenomenal shape. He is a long-time cycler and he has even competed in triathlons. Dr. Jack is incredibly intense, and he takes every game hard, Paxson said, but the next morning he has a good workout and is ready to go. That's what I'm saying. You've got to have some outlet. With K.C., it was singing. He'd seek out a piano bar and belt out "You're Nobody 'Till Somebody Loves You" a few times, and he'd feel better.

You've got to get hold of your emotions and channel them into something besides basketball. I played golf a dozen times or so with Rick Carter when he coached at Holy Cross. He would talk about nothing but football. I'm not really interested in football. The man was totally preoccupied with football and had no sense of humor.

Carter ended up hanging himself. Apparently, he thought the big opportunities were passing him by. Going 11-0 at Holy Cross wasn't good enough. He motivated his kids well because he had that kind of complete dedication to a responsibility, and he certainly had his impact on the players. He was highly successful in terms of wins and losses, but perhaps he never added enough other things to his life, including his own family.

When it comes to the job, how much can you do? You hear about coaches—it used to be football coaches exclusively, but now it's spread to basketball—who boast about how "I can outwork any sumbitch out there." What does it mean? You can only look at the game tapes so many times. You watch the opponents, and you get a handle on what their basic plays are. You see them hold up two fingers, and you and your assistant know what play that means. You can only hope your players remember what you told them.

A coach has got to create an atmosphere where the players are not inhibited. You don't want to restrict their talent by frightening them, and yet you want to create an atmosphere where you get the proper respect in the player–coach relationship. Then you stay away from them. Basketball makes it very easy to overcoach. Generally speaking, let the situation develop on the floor. Don't inject yourself or your ego into something that doesn't require it.

In college, coach a little bit more. Still, the coaches who stand up in high school, college, and the pros and call a play every time down the floor don't understand they are inhibiting the natural talent of their players. In other sports this may not be the case, but in basketball I think by trying to implement your book knowledge at every turn you too often wind up being counterproductive.

A good coach has got to be flexible in many ways. For years the Utah Jazz were a real two-platoon team. Frank Layden used nine or ten men all the time. This year, they became a seven-man team. During the playoffs he got it down to six, unless he was in foul trouble.

I respect a coach with that kind of flexibility because that's what it's all about. You can't come in, especially at the NBA level, with a set of guidelines, principles, and philosophies and stuff them down everyone's throats because of your ego. Some people are stubborn. They say, in effect, "I don't care whether or not my material fits what I'm trying to do. This is the way it's going to be done." The smart coach is the one who doesn't let his ego interfere and who is flexible enough to do one thing this year and something else the next, depending on the identity of the personnel and the overall situation. That's the practical approach.

I don't think you can use flat-out fear as a motivator. Even at BC, where you probably *could* scare the kids, I didn't approach it that way. I used to spend a long time with a hand-chosen captain because I felt if I could get my priorities across to him and put the responsibilities on his shoulders, he could articulate what I wanted in the privacy of the locker room. Then it would make my job a hell of a lot easier, and I wouldn't have to wind up screaming to make the same point to the team.

I think today's athlete will still respond to a sincere, genuine approach by a coach, who, presumably, they have the proper respect for. You no longer can frighten them. When you try to use scare tactics, players either reject you or file a grievance with the Players Association. What weapons do you have? You've got to use more subtle techniques.

— 7 —

More Motivation

THERE ARE TIMES when you can X and O yourself to death. One night last year, the Celtics were down ten points in Milwaukee. We were broadcasting from next to the bench. I was looking at the five guys, and not one of them was paying attention to K.C. You talk about instinctively knowing what to do.

What was K.C. doing? He had the clipboard out there and he was drawing plays. Ten down with two minutes to go, and he's diagramming plays? That is not germane to the situation. At that point, you've got to go out and kill. You've got to go out and pressure. There isn't much you can accomplish diagramming plays.

This is the modern coaching approach, and it doesn't make any sense. The idea is to go out and play the game. Guys like Bill Fitch spend hours and hours looking at film. I would reject that. I don't want to keep picking on him because in most respects he's an excellent coach. But I saw him close up for four years. If I were to go back into coaching, I would reject completely this approach. (Something, I believe, Doug Moe has already done.) I would reject the little blackboard in the huddle. Every coach now seems to feel he's got to go into that huddle with that blackboard. Why? Insecurity. The others are doing it, so I had better do it too. I know the players sit there and ignore it. I know players sit in darkened rooms during practice and ignore the tapes. It is all a waste of time. I can think of nothing more useless than being in that huddle, down 10, with two minutes to go. At that point you must provide emotional stimulus, not X's and O's.

I've been concerned about the motivation and determination of the Celtics for some time. Many a day last season I talked with K.C. on the day of a game, asking him what was on his mind, what kind of technical adjustments he was thinking about. He'd say, "We've got to rebound. We've got to start controlling the boards on the road. We've got guys now that all figure they're All Stars, so let someone else do the dirty work. Everybody thinks he can shoot us back into the game. We have to go for the rebound and get the second and third shot more often."

K.C. had lost the ability to communicate with players. The time had come when they needed a stimulus, and he wasn't able to provide it. This is a natural phenomenon, especially when a team has enjoyed the success the Celtics have. I don't think the players consciously turned K.C. off, but they weren't responding, just the same.

K.C. is black and insecure. More than anything else, this probably has kept him from receiving his proper due and recognition over the years for both his playing and his coaching accomplishments. K.C. has always played it laid back and low key in an attempt to hide from the spotlight he'd rather not be in. Despite having been very successful at just about every level of sports he's participated in, he's never received the credit he deserves.

I agree with those who say that nothing works for long with today's professional athlete. Change for the sake of change is the way to go. Follow the hard line of Bill Fitch that was extremely successful for three years with the K.C. "nice guy" approach for the next three before the troops need new stimulation once again. There are those who say the Celtics sensed this need to change and gently moved K.C. upstairs with a generous six-year contract at a time when it had become Jimmy Rodgers's turn. In my judgment, it was an excellent move for all concerned.

K.C. probably would have preferred to coach for another three or four years, but it was time for a change, and the change was handled properly. He goes out with his head held high, his accomplishments in place. He has earned championship rings as a player and a coach. At some time in the privacy of his living room he can finally boast a bit to his grandchildren about the significant role he played in Celtics history. He'd never do it publicly.

Now Jimmy Rodgers has the opportunity he's long waited and prepared for, one that was denied him a year ago when the Knickerbockers asked to interview him for their coaching job. And of course it gives the boys on the Celtics a new voice and personality to focus on. Rodgers is technically sound and well prepared. He'll make a few personnel changes, but generally he'll continue to implement the Celtic philosophy. Will he make a difference? Can he coax one more championship ring out of an aging and declining team before the Bird era is over? His success will depend more on his powers of persuasion and motivation, in my opinion, than on his coaching or bench expertise. He must find a way to light a sustained fire rather than an occasional one. He must give the senior players a reason to give it "one more try" with a 100 percent effort. They're still the best five in the NBA for brief periods of time. Rodgers must not let the tail wag the dog. He must call the shots completely on who plays when and for how long. He must involve the young players in the games so they push and inspire the veterans. If the youngsters can't produce, it won't work, and the downward cycle will continue. But we don't know that yet, and playing them is the only viable option (unless Arnold has yet one more rabbit to pull out of the hat).

It is improbable and definitely a long shot, but with the talent that's left on the Celtics, led by Bird and McHale, with a strong "goose" by some eager and talented young players, and with new inspirational leadership, the Mystique might work one more time and produce championship number 17.

Jimmy Rodgers came in talking about being a stickler for detail. I hope he follows through. There were many examples of the team being unwilling to focus on the small things that make the difference in games, especially on the road. The team often gets away with playing unsound basketball because a Bird or McHale is there to take over a game long enough to turn it around. But you can't live on that. Ainge will throw up those three-pointers, and I'll get on him on the air. I get letters about my criticisms. People say they are tired of hearing about it. They'll say, "We know Danny shouldn't be taking them, but do we have to listen to you all the time?" But what can I do? There are times the team will be lucky to make two passes on a trip down the floor. Or we'll start off going inside with great success for the first two or three minutes and then forget it for the next forty. Then it's "Christ, we are going to lose this game, so let's get it inside."

The Celtics' inattention to detail is reflected in careless passing or in failure to fight for proper position in the post. Sometimes McHale will have guys clawing all over him when he's on offense, but when he gets down to the other end, he just plants himself behind his man and allows an easy entry pass. He knows better than that. It reflects the general attitude that they are not willing, for whatever reason, to pay the price, given the situation.

Even so, the team can still win games. There was a game in Atlanta last year that was absolutely given away by the Hawks. You almost wished the Celtics lost it. They would have been better off, rather than thinking the effort they put forth that night was deserving of a victory.

I've talked about the path of least resistance. I remain convinced that it is the favorite thoroughfare of just about every player in just about every situation. If they think they can bust their asses for a quarter and get away with it, that is what they will do. The Celtics have done that for a year and a half now. You can date their turnaround to February of 1987. They came home from a successful Western Conference trip, and ever since then they have been spotty on the road. They don't have the determination.

But it's hard to impress on these guys what's really important and what isn't if the proper signals aren't sent. One of my biggest shocks in all my years in the league came a few years ago when both the players and K.C. himself brought not only their wives, but also their children to Los Angeles during the Finals. I cannot to this day imagine Arnold sanctioning such a thing. Here they were talking about going to Disneyland the day before the game. K.C. had his baby there. What are the players supposed to think?

There was Kevin McHale pushing the stroller around the pool at the Marriott when the team was trying to concentrate on beating the Lakers. That's a far cry from

Bob Cousy barricading himself in his hotel room, having all his meals sent up and thinking about little except his opponent the day of a playoff game. Granted, my approach may have been a little extreme, even for the times, but this other extreme was unimaginable.

From a coaching standpoint, objecting to having the wives and kiddies at the hotel during the Finals dates me. But I assure you I wouldn't allow it. How much common sense does that make to you? For Christ's sake, you work eight months for this culmination. You can't work another ten days and focus completely? You should limit any outside distractions. You're there for the game. Having your wife *and* baby there? Incredible.

I'm only a broadcaster, and even I need to get focused on the day of a game. I get my rest, and I go over my notes and think about what I'm going to say. I minimize distractions, and that's just to *analyze* the game. As a player, how many things can you concentrate on and function to maximum capacity?

Maybe it's just my particular phobia. I used to do my Garbo thing during the playoffs in the last two or three years of my career. I'd get away from distractions and just stay in my room. I'd have my meals sent up because I wanted to avoid dealing with the public in any way, and I'd focus on getting my mind set properly. When you're young, it happens automatically. In those days, I didn't have to work at getting myself up for the game. I could get myself up for a three-on-three game. As you get older, it's more difficult. You have to work at it. And today there are many more forces pulling you.

Today you get strollers at the pool. That's why I think the Celtics needed another voice. They needed the Steinbrenner way: Bring in a voice players will listen to, and get a momentary impact. When that wears off, bring in another voice. With all of that said, on balance I think K.C.'s approach was very successful and exactly what was needed at the time. Forces were at work that no one can control for long periods of time in professional sports today. The tail is wagging the dog.

Now that I've grown up, I realize I was like those CEOs you read about. I was so into achievement while moving up the ladder that I lost precious years with my wife and kids. Where were my priorities? I will never be able to make up those years I missed with my daughters. But the competition is so severe that, unfortunately, you've got to give complete commitment to whatever it is you want to do. Other things will suffer. You look back and say, yes, my personal side should have been more important. Now I'm trying to make up.

I keep asking myself how Auerbach permits some of the things that go on with the Celtics, but he's learned to roll with the punches. He has compromised. He has projected that tough, hard-nosed image, but his bark is worse than his bite. That he's made everything work is proof he's the glue that holds the Celtics together. The young players still think he is tough, even though he is not as tough as he sounds.

There is something very powerful about Auerbach's presence. Years ago, Dave Cowens said it would be very strange ever to walk into Auerbach's office and not see him. He said he felt better about everything just seeing him there. Arnold has always been able to transmit that confidence to his troops. Even when we weren't big winners, we were generally overachieving, or, at least, playing as well as we could, simply because Big Brother was there.

The Celtics have always known that Auerbach would fight for them. That in itself takes the pressure off the troops. Thank God you don't have to shake hands with the opposition after an NBA game. I don't think Arnold would ever have done that. He's not a gracious loser. That's all right with me. If I'm going to hire a coach, I want the son of a bitch to be a sore loser. That's the guy who's going to be successful.

One of the interesting problems in basketball is how to deal with the superior individual player. What you decide to accomplish with such a player gets right to the heart of basketball's eternal essence; there are five people and one basketball.

Isn't it fascinating, for example, that the Celtics won eleven championships with Bill Russell and Kareem Abdul-Jabbar has won six titles, but Wilt Chamberlain, perhaps the most physically gifted big man of them all, won only two? I've spoken about Russell, and why I feel there is no question about his superiority as a player to Chamberlain. There is clearly a lesson to be learned when you compare Kareem, who is far more of an offensive player than Russell ever was, to Chamberlain.

Keeping everyone involved offensively is the goal. As a playmaker, I knew I couldn't expect those big guys to bust their asses defensively and on the boards unless I paid them back at the other end. A coach has to integrate all the available offensive and defensive factors. From the very beginning, Larry Costello's tenure with Kareem was so much easier than anyone's was with Chamberlain. You were so restricted with Wilt. For years he couldn't hit a free man if he was standing right in front of him. Your halfcourt offense becomes much more productive with Kareem than with Wilt. Kareem is a constant problem because he always has that hook. In coaching against him, you try to create different traps, and you try to mix up where they're coming from, but Kareem generally finds the right open man, anyway.

When you have a player who is a prolific scorer but

who can also execute the pinpoint pass in the halfcourt, it puts massive pressure on the defense. And if you're the offense, you're more inclined to wait for that kind of player to come back upcourt after the ball changes hands. In Wilt's case, the reverse was true. I would never have told the other four guys to wait for Wilt. I'd try to run the break every time I could. That's not the way it worked out, of course.

When Milwaukee won the championship in 1971, they did it with forwards who were 6′6″ and 6′5″. They had Bob Dandridge, who was young and frisky, and they had Greg Smith, a roadrunner who would play defense. Those forwards got out and ran. Meanwhile, Kareem was scoring a casual thirty-four points a game. Everybody was happy because they had a constant up-tempo game. Milwaukee, incidentally, was the first team ever to shoot fifty percent from the floor. One reason they did so was Kareem's accuracy. A second reason was the open jump shots created by Kareem's presence in the halfcourt. A third reason was the sheer volume of easy layups they got as a result of Kareem's rebounding. (He rebounded well for the first ten years he was in the league.)

It's not easy for the average big man to learn how to pass from the low hole. You've got to sense the pressure if it's coming from behind, and there's a lot going on. Kevin McHale has gradually learned what it's all about, but it did not come naturally. The other players used to kid him, saying that throwing the ball in there was like watching it disappear into the Black Hole. But Kareem knew what he was doing from Year One. He immediately looked to the weak side when the ball came in. You always seemed to be giving up layups, rather than 16-footers.

The point is that Kareem is going to burn you, so having him in the hole in every aspect of the game gives a coach so much more flexibility than having Wilt in there. Wilt really restricted you.

Coaches must fight the temptation to rely excessively on a player like Wilt to generate individual offense. Wilt once scored 100 points in a game. He once averaged 50 points a game for a season. Kareem has always had that spectacular hook shot. Each time down the floor, logic dictates that the most efficient way of getting the ball in the basket is to give it to the big guy and get out of his way. The Chicago Bulls are facing that dilemma with Michael Jordan today. It's very tempting to say, "Michael, go one-on-one about thirty times today."

It doesn't work that way. There are four other players on the court, and they must be involved. The psychology of the game precludes the possibility of lasting success by relying on one person to score. If all that person can do is shoot, the idea is even more ridiculous.

The fact that we can discuss Kareem Abdul-Jabbar in the present tense is rather amazing, especially for someone who remembers him in high school and who coached against him in college. I even "recruited" Kareem for BC, although he didn't know it.

That was a weird story. Kareem's—I should say Lew Alcindor's—coach in high school was Jack Donohue, a prototypical New Yorker who has been the head coach of the Canadian national team for many years and has done a helluva good job for Canadian basketball. Donohue has the gift of gab, and one day he called me up out of the blue and said that Lew Alcindor was interested in Boston College. Great, I figured.

I subsequently found out that Jack Donohue was interested in the Holy Cross job, and at some point he came to me and asked for whatever help I could give him. Given my basic cynicism, it didn't take long to put two and two together, but I played along with it and wrote the necessary letters. Then Donohue told me he was handling the kid and he didn't want anyone to have any personal contact with Lew. This went on for a couple of weeks. Finally, I insisted that Donohue give me Lew's phone number.

I called him. Hell, he didn't know anything about Boston College. He had no intention of coming to BC. It's a good thing I hadn't really taken the whole thing seriously. Incidentally, with or without my help, and I didn't give much, Jack Donohue got the job at Holy Cross.

How Kareem has lasted this long is remarkable. One reason he's been able to stay in the NBA as long as he has is the fact that he isn't particularly intense, not, for example, the way Russell was. Without a certain mental approach, he could never have had this type of career. This is a paradox. Kareem probably combined the respective strengths of both Russell and Chamberlain in one physical package, without ever becoming as effective in some areas as he might have been. But his attitude has enabled him to play into his forties. I think he would have burned out much earlier if he had played with Russell's intensity.

Kareem does not have Russell's speed and quickness getting up and down the floor, but he has size, reach, and intelligence. He has the instincts to be Russell's equal as a shot blocker, but not the interest. And he certainly could have been a better rebounder than he's been.

Kareem's rebounding bugs some people, but Pat Riley has adjusted to it, and he's the one who has to live with it. I buy Riley's approach. He's not fazed by it. By this time, Riley knows what he's getting. He knows he's better off molding the other players' talents and his personality to the existing game plan, rather than trying to change the individual.

Riley appears to be very good at dealing with delicate

psyches. Basketball is a very simple game at its core, but it has its complexities. I can safely say that at this point in time it's better to have a shrink sitting next to you on the bench than a trainer, because you need a logical understanding of personalities and psyches to create the desired chemistry on a ball club.

As much as you may need to get the players up during the regular season, you may need to calm them down during the playoffs. There are times you can clearly have *too* much emotion.

— 8 —

Coaching
College Basketball

If it's true that you have a very difficult time finding a sufficient number of people entering professional basketball with the values of a selfless team player, I can tell you why. It's because they come out of a cesspool known as college athletics.

I was a part of the collegiate system for six years what seems like a very long time ago. Talk about the Age of Innocence, compared to what we know today . . . when I was at Boston College the players were still voting to go to either the NCAA tournament or the NIT, by virtue of the fact that New York was still viewed as the mecca of basketball, and Madison Square Garden, old and new, was considered *the* place to perform. We were just reaching the point where the NCAA tournament was clearly the more meaningful of the two. I know that if you're under thirty, you have a difficult time comprehending this, given the grandiose state of the NCAA tournament today.

Of course, in those days there wasn't any question who was going to win the NCAA tournament. At least the NIT had legitimate competition. I'm talking about the mid- to late-sixties, when it was UCLA vs. the world. You knew deep down you weren't going to win it, so you gave real consideration to going into the NIT. It's entirely different now. Everybody wants to go to the NCAA tournament. If you don't make the tournament, it is considered to be some sort of disgrace. They have 64 teams in the tournament (there were 25 when we at BC first went in 1967), and whoever thinks he is number 65 is ready to get a lawyer and sue for the opportunity to get in. It doesn't matter how diluted the tournament is, people must have it on their record that they've gone to the NCAA tourney. The NIT was a pretty nice tournament, and it's been destroyed in the process. Oh, it still carries on. They play regionally until the semifinals, when the remaining four games come to New York. Tell me how many recent NIT champions you can name. Go ahead.

The motivating factor is that famed five-letter word: M-O-N-E-Y. You get $250,000 for getting into the NCAA tournament. That's team number 64. Those fortunate enough to get to the Final Four receive in excess of a million dollars each. And people wonder why there is such rampant cheating?

The temptation to cheat selectively is great in basketball because it doesn't take much to turn a team around. In football the name of the game is numbers. Attrition takes its toll. There may be fifty or seventy teams that can line up on a Saturday afternoon and defeat a top five team—once. But that team might sustain a few injuries and be unable to defeat a team in the eighty to one hundred range the following week. When Nebraska loses a starting offensive tackle, the system is geared to produce a replacement who is just as good as the guy he replaces. This is not rhetoric, as any student of college football knows.

You don't need great numbers in basketball. A superstar player, properly complemented by happily subservient, aggressive teammates can take a team a long way. Larry Bird took just such an Indiana State team to the NCAA Finals in 1979. Danny Manning went one better in 1988, leading a Kansas team not overburdened with first round draft choices to the championship. Take Manning away and where would that injury-stricken Kansas team have been? Probably second division in the Big Eight. And yet with one exceptional player in charge, Kansas won the whole thing. That's the lure of basketball, and it's why *everybody* dreams of achieving great things.

The system isn't geared to bring out the best in anybody. Most people don't ask if the ends justify the means; they already have made up their minds on that topic. The game was sick enough when I coached at Boston College between 1963 and 1969, but that was almost a kind of prehistoric chapter in the life and times of NCAA Division I basketball, compared with what is going on today.

How are kids supposed to know the difference between right and wrong, when all they are exposed to half the time is wrong and wronger? What kind of role models can the coaches be when they have become the biggest collection of hoboes and vagabonds in American life today? Just about every coach is eyeing another job. It is one segment of the society where the grass *always* seems to be greener elsewhere. When Kansas hired North Carolina assistant Roy Williams to replace outgoing head coach Larry Brown, Williams announced at the press conference that the school wouldn't need another one of these gatherings for thirty years. I'd like to believe him, but somehow I know better. With the exception of Dean Smith, Digger Phelps, and John Thompson, coaches aren't sticking around schools very long these days. There always seems to be another place where the tumblers are in place to "get it done."

A kid who has entered college under shady pretenses—accepting money, cars, jobs for family members, and God-knows-what as an inducement to enroll—winds up being handled by a coach who may very well have left his last stop a half-step ahead of the recruiting violations posse. Is this the blind leading the blind, or what?

It eludes me how coaches are allowed to go skipping from job to job, leaving a trail of investigations behind them. If a college is caught in a violation, the coach and/or athletic director has got to go. You've got to put the pressure on the administrators and coaches, and not just the kids.

I feel very strongly about this. The offending school can't just be made to pay a fine. You have got to make the penalties apply to the individuals who are responsible for those violations, who are now planning a move to the next school where the process can repeat itself all over again. What happens here? The school loses a few bucks during a probation period. It's usually worth the gamble. North Carolina State was on probation for recruiting violations during the 1972–73 season. The next year, the illegally recruited players won the national championship. I'm sure the folks down in Raleigh thought it was a good deal overall. How many schools in America would forfeit a chance to win the title in 1989 if they believed they had a terrific chance to win the big prize in 1990, using those same players?

The NCAA has got to make the penalties serious enough to affect not only the pocketbook of the school, but also the careers of the coaches and athletic directors who are creating these violations. I favor giving the athlete a second chance. It's obvious they are being corrupted by a system that has established this whole spectrum of violations as part of the game.

*   *   *

Everyone cheats to some degree. You are dealing with seventeen-year olds who are learning how to cheat. They are being told it is okay to violate rules, whatever the rules happen to be. They see what's going on because they are the prime beneficiaries. The coaches and athletic directors condone the activities of nefarious "boosters," many of whom are corrupting these kids.

Some have offered as a solution the idea of paying the kids a stipend. Put the money on the table. The problem here is that the schools who wanted players the most would find a way to pay the most money. I think you'd create an even bigger monster by legalizing payments. And I just don't think you can rely on the NCAA to police itself. I think you may have to take some of the money made available by the NCAA tournament and the television funds to create an objective, independent police force. Whatever is done, there has got to be a very stern penalty against individuals, not just the institutions.

We all got an idea of how pervasive the corruption can get during the public examination of the SMU situation. Here you had everyone involved, from the governor of Texas on down. We are talking football here, but if we were in a few other states we could be talking basketball. There is an unbelievable keeping-up-with-the Joneses mentality in the state of Texas when the subject is the athletic program of the alma mater.

I was speaking at a small college somewhere in Texas five or six years ago and a guy came up to me afterwards. The coach had told me before I spoke to stroke this guy, and here he came. He was a Texan sent right over from central casting: the boots, the Stetson, the works.

He said, "Goddamn it, coach, what can I do? I am

spending all this money. I fly these kids around. It is not enough. What can I do to attract people to this little town? We can't compete with the Dallases and the Houstons. What can I do? I'll spend whatever it takes. I'll get them girls, anything they want." He then went through the litany of everything that was going on. He said that everybody else in their conference was doing it, and I'm sure they were. He said, "We are prepared to do it. What can I do to give us an edge on the other guys?" The point is that it's not a question of a few people doing it. They *all* do it to some degree, with few exceptions, unfortunately.

The Southwest Conference recently had five or six schools on probation in football. That's incredible. They don't care because down there football is the state religion. It's the same as knowing that we all cheat on our income taxes, to some degree. When enough people feel that everyone else is doing it, they figure if they play it straight, what chance do they have? Everyone else is cheating on their income tax, so I'll cheat just a little on mine.

That is the thinking that has gone on for years in college recruiting. I must cheat to be successful. The amount of cheating, or the seriousness of the offense, is directly related to the size of the program and the amount of money at stake. The small schools cheat a little bit and the big guys cheat a lot.

It's so very tempting because if you get yourself those one or two special players, off you'll go, into the Associated Press Top Twenty.

There is a general impatience in society anyway. Doing things the old, slow, solid way is no longer in vogue. Is there any doubt that we are living in the Age of Instant Gratification? Look at the takeover guys on Wall Street. They're out to double their investment in three or four months. The principle applies across the board.

Forget the jock for a minute. The kid getting out of college wants to start at a $40,000 job. New graduates don't want to hear about building themselves up for twenty years, and then making some serious money.

There's pressure on everybody at all times. College, pro, probably even high school. People are reluctant to speak in cautious terms. No one thinks he or she can afford to be anything but instantly effective. When Willis Reed took over the New Jersey Nets last season, I read with interest his remarks. "This isn't a dead situation," was the gist of it. The truth is there are few things deader than that franchise. That is going to be a dead situation for the next ten years. It doesn't matter if it's Willis Reed or anyone else. But he's got to be excessively upbeat. You and I know the situation is not going to change.

It's no different in college. A guy gets hired at a school that has broken .500 once in ten years and that hasn't been to either major tournament since Ike was president, and he's got more optimism than a TV evangelist. The coach steps up and says he can do it. He'd *better* be able to do it because the college president tells him he's got an X million dollar athletic budget to sustain, and alumni contributions have fallen off and we have been mediocre for too long. A quick change is needed. The pressure is on. How do you get quick change?

You go into junior colleges and buy players. That's what you've got to do. The fans and administrators don't have the patience to allow a new coach a reasonable amount of time to turn the program around.

The whole thing has accelerated to an unimaginable degree. I began coaching in 1963 after retiring from the Celtics. I made $12,000 a year. Fortunately, I had other sources of income. Of course, it wasn't a full-time job either.

Today, college coaching is a 12-month commitment. Back then recruiting was more haphazard. My name helped attract a number of good eastern ballplayers to BC at first. We had the usual alumni contacts. And there was my summer camp in Pittsfield, N.H., which helped me cheat. That's right, I said cheat.

While I was at BC, I used to invite high school seniors to my camp. I wasn't allowed to do it, but I did it. I tried to get around the NCAA regulations by putting them on the staff. The rule was clear. You couldn't have high school seniors. I wasn't real proud of myself, but I felt I needed that little edge because in many other ways —full-time assistants, for example—BC had not given me the tools to compete with the other schools we dealt with.

I never felt pressure in my first two years at BC. We went 10–11 the first year, and then got rolling with a 22–7 record, a fifteen-game winning streak, and a berth in the NIT (only BC's second trip ever until then) the second year. But the third year, we had to maintain that turnaround. Thank God, we did (21–5 and the NIT again). I really felt more pressure that third year to succeed. I knew despite the fact that BC had never given me squat in terms of tools to work with that maybe I could do it if I succumbed to the pressure to bend the rules in some manner. Eventually, I left. I was the so-called guy who walked away. But I'm a product of that environment, just like so many others. It all depends on what price it will take to make you prostitute yourself.

College basketball is 100 percent hypocrisy. With the money available today from the NCAA tournament, who wouldn't chance breaking the rules? The guideline is that the end does justify the means. You do whatever you have to do to be successful, and if you get caught, you cop out.

It's not as if coaches twenty or thirty years ago didn't

do whatever they felt was necessary to win. In those days, they weren't bound by the stringent scholarship restrictions in force today. Perhaps you've heard about the old recruiting practices at Alabama, where they would bring in ten, twelve, or fifteen top-flight high school quarterbacks a year and let them fight it out. That kind of thing was going on in basketball, too.

When BC played Tennessee at the 1966 Sugar Bowl Tournament, I found myself chatting with Tennessee coach Ray Mears. In the course of conversation, he mentioned he had recruited twelve point guards that year. Twelve point guards? I couldn't believe that. That doesn't mean he wound up offering all of them scholarships. He was speaking of actively recruiting them, but just the same, twelve point guards? I didn't recruit twelve point guards in my six years at BC, I am sure, let alone twelve in one recruiting year.

Mears was operating in a different stratosphere than I was. Tennessee was the master of the hard sell. Once, we actually outrecruited a large conference school down South for a player. The kid told us about the plane landing at the airport, the red carpet literally being rolled out for him, the female escorts stepping right up, and the dramatic announcement at the game of his visit to the school. Later he told me, "Coach, if you'd spent a recruiting trip like I did, you wouldn't ask why I considered that school." That kind of experience happened to a lot of kids. I wonder where their heads were after weekends like *that*?

My basic approach was to zero in on a kid we had a realistic chance to recruit and say, "If you come to BC, that's your position. We won't recruit another player for the job." That was it. If a kid said he'd come to BC, we backed off other choices.

Now, perhaps if you're at Tennessee or a comparable school and your resources are different, then your approach is, too. With that kind of muscle and access to kids, you change your priorities. I always wanted to start from outside in, with sound point guards to run my offense. But I never found the need, or had the resources, to simultaneously recruit twelve of them.

Depth is nice, but how many good players do you need? Some coaches today—Jim Valvano of North Carolina State comes to mind—are notorious for "over-recruiting." All they wind up with are unhappy people and a bunch of players transferring to different schools.

I was once in such a situation, but as a player, not a coach. My first coach at Holy Cross was Alvain "Doggie" Julian. In those days you really didn't "recruit" anyone. Doggie sent out letters of interest, and maybe a guy showed up and maybe he didn't. Well, this was right after World War II, and in my first year, a lot of guys showed up. Doggie wound up with ten guys who could probably start for any team in the country at that time.

We all wanted to play, and Doggie wasn't quite sure how to handle it. He was basically a football coach with some experience coaching basketball. He was a *laissez-faire* coach. Our star player, George Kaftan, used to tease him during practice. Doggie had this habit of rubbing our foreheads for luck before games, and Kaftan would then rub Doggie's nose to loosen things up. Doggie's problem was keeping all this talent involved, so he two-platooned. Except that it was automatic. Exactly nine and a half minutes into the game Bob Curran, the team's oldest player and co-captain with Ken Haggerty, would get up, no matter what was going on out there, and lead us into the game. Just like that. We'd check in (I was a freshman) and play the next ten minutes.

This is the way it went until the NCAA tournament, at which point Doggie knew in his heart he should whittle it down to seven or eight guys. We won the NCAA tournament, and I don't think we would have won it with the platoon system. That's the last time I was mixed up in anything like that. Buster Sheary came in the next year, and then I played for Arnold. They all substituted individually.

Having an overabundance of talent was not usually one of my problems at BC. I was a novice when I took that job. I knew nothing about recruiting. I hadn't even been through the recruiting process myself. I am fond of saying I was deluged by two college offers, and it's the truth, despite being all-city in New York.

I was isolated completely for thirteen years. I thought it was fun and games. I thought you invited someone to the Celtics game, and you signed him the next day. We actually did that with John Austin, a guard from Washington, D.C. Arnold, who lives in D.C. and falls in love with any player with the remotest Washington connection, helped me get Austin. He turned out to be an outstanding player for us.

I guess the impact of my name helped us to get guards such as Billy Evans (New Haven, Conn.) and Jimmy O'Brien (Brooklyn, N.Y.). We were very lucky with Terry Driscoll, who we recruited from Boston College High School as a 6'5" center with baby fat. He wound up being the MVP of the 1969 NIT, and the fourth pick in the NBA draft.

My freshman coach was Frank Power, and he had many New England contacts, as well as friends throughout New York, New Jersey, and Pennsylvania. If we didn't have Frank, I don't know what we would have done. Probably the best eastern kid we ever recruited was a 6'8" forward from Chaminade High on Long Island named Jim Kissane. When we got him, I was convinced we had an All-American and a definite NBA player. Jimmy was an intelligent kid, but kind of a head case. He had a lot of leaping ability and quickness, but he never developed as he should have. He was his own worst enemy.

It wasn't so much that we felt we were thrown in

with the wolves at BC. We had limited financial resources and we were low key compared to many of the
other schools. I had the camp, and I used to invite kids
I was after. The thing I learned was that the most important inducement—and I'm not certain this isn't true
today—is playing time. Kids want to know what their
chances are of playing, even more than what other things
are in it for them.

I would make that commitment. I'd always qualify
it by saying, "It's still up to you. You have to produce,
but if you do your job, the opportunity is here. You won't
be fighting four other guys for your position. There
won't be twelve point guards, or eight big forwards, or
ten centers."

I coached in the era of noneligibility for freshmen,
and I endorse that concept. If you put the priorities in
place, even the superstars can use one year of adjustment to college life, be it academic, social, or other
ways. Players can get acclimated to the pressures they
will be subjected to, if, in fact, they are blue-chippers.
Take a year to get prepared, and then you can be a
big gun.

There are more factors. By not having freshmen el-
igible, you are not infringing on the egos of the seniors
who have put three or four years into the program,
establishing an identity. You're not threatening what
older kids have earned by elevating a freshman with
superior physical talent. It's all too much on the younger
kid's system.

Freshman noneligibility is therapeutic in both senses.
It's humbling for the freshman, which establishes a
firmer foundation for him, and it doesn't threaten the
kids who have worked and at least deserve that last
year of exposure.

Nobody talks about this. For every Mark Macon or
J.R. Reid there have been a hundred or a thousand

freshmen who weren't ready to play. In the current circumstance, if you bring in the highly sought-after guy, he wants to be the big cheese—now. That's part of your commitment when you bring him in.

But it's not going to change. Freshman teams cost money, and that's the bottom line. Moreoever, some kids are talented enough to step in and make a real difference in team performance. They might even help a team advance far into the NCAA tournament to make even more money. That's sports in America, college or pro. It's so obvious everyone would be better off if they made freshmen sit out a year. It would be better for the seniors, better for the freshmen, and better for everyone in between. But they'll never do it.

— 9 —

College Basketball
and Bobby Knight

BACK IN THE '50s, I did a book with Al Hirshberg. I said there was something wrong with this society. I said we were making heroes out of our jocks by placing them on pedestals. First we put them up there, and when they display their clay feet we throw stones at them.

Jocks don't deserve to be there, I said. People were planning on going to the moon and doing any number of other meaningful things, and we paid no attention. It was true then, and it is true now.

Nikita Khrushchev said, "We don't have to bury you; you'll bury yourselves." He knew about the avarice and greed that pervade our win-at-all-costs society. In sports, we see it reflected in the behavior of our sports administrators and coaches. In society, we see it in some corrupt cops, politicians, and business leaders. In sports it all starts with recruiting. We are corrupting young, impressionable people before they even get to college. Over a decade ago, John Devaney and I interviewed Sonny Vaccaro, a man knowledgeable in the area of high school and college athletics. He said every kid he had known at a major school who had gone through the hardcore recruiting process was "on the take, in one form or another."

College presidents don't participate in basketball recruiting, but neither did Richard Nixon "participate" in Watergate. He knew what was going on, and college presidents know what's going on. The pros say they want to win and make money. The colleges have the same objectives, but they spout high-falutin' gobbledygook about "higher education."

I entered college coaching differently than most people, because I was Bob Cousy of the Boston Celtics, not a guy trying to make it up through the ranks. I was naive and idealistic. I wanted to win, and I wanted to do it the right way. I knew people would be looking closely at what I did and how I did it. I believed what the Jesuits had told me: It doesn't matter whether you win or lose but how you play the game. I was grabbed by the romanticism of it all. Work with kids. Teach some basketball. And make it to the tournament to make the fans happy.

After a while, you realize what it takes to win. Any person with a conscience knows right from wrong. We don't need priests or society to tell us how to live. You know when you are getting into problem areas. Coming out of the New York ghetto, I had well-honed survival instincts. I have exploited every situation since then. I was never unaware for a second of the positive benefits of being Bob Cousy, *Boston Celtic.*

I always maintained a very credible, positive image. I worked hard at it. I wanted to be viewed as a nice guy. Did I succeed? Who knows? I am not the judge.

The point is that I created the image, and I was, and am, very anxious to hold onto it. That's why when *Life* magazine came out with a story in 1967 smearing me for having underworld connections it destroyed me. Today, I would thumb my nose at the world. We see that kind of "indictment by innuendo" all the time today in the pages of publications such as the *National Enquirer*. That article almost destroyed me, but I overcame it.

All of us give ourselves the benefit of the doubt. It depends on what is at stake. I have been pressured from time to time because of things I've said in my broadcasts. We are told we have been "too negative" for the last year or two. Well, the fact is that the Celtics underachieved all last year. My general manager, Gerry Walsh of Channel 56 in Boston, is conscious of his responsibility to the Celtics as well as to the viewer. I told him I thought our main responsibility was to the credibility of the broadcast. It is possible to do a positive broadcast without compromising our integrity. I don't think I have ever compromised my principles on these broadcasts, and I don't intend to start now.

There is greed everywhere. We are all making judgments. The fact is that many of us, in all walks of life, are subject to peer pressure. They caught those cops in New York, the ones written about in Mike McAlary's book *Buddy Boys*. What did they say when they were caught? "Yeah, I'm a cop. Yeah, I know the difference between right and wrong. But if everybody in the station house is doing it, why shouldn't I?"

Honesty in public life doesn't seem to count for much either. Look at politics. The only candidate for president in 1988 who came out and said we have got to raise taxes was Bruce Babbit. You saw where it got him. If you are honest and candid, you will never get elected. That is the tragedy of our society. Too often to accomplish a purpose, you have to cheat and lie to the people.

Little situations crop up all the time, putting you on the defensive. A guy called me last year and said he

I am looking to pass to Russ, as usual, in the Boston Garden.

This is my first Celtic team and Arnold's, too. Those in the picture are (*front, from left*) Ken Sailors, Bob Donham, Sonny Hertzberg, Bob Cousy, Ed Leede, and Coach Red Auerbach; (*rear*) Ed Stanczak, Chuck Cooper, Harry Boykhoff, Andy Duncan, Brady Walker, John Mahnken, and Easy Ed Macauley. (William Meikie, *The Boston Traveler*)

My wife, Marie, and our daughters Mary Patricia (*left*) and Marie Collette are ready to skate while I observe. (*The Boston Herald*)

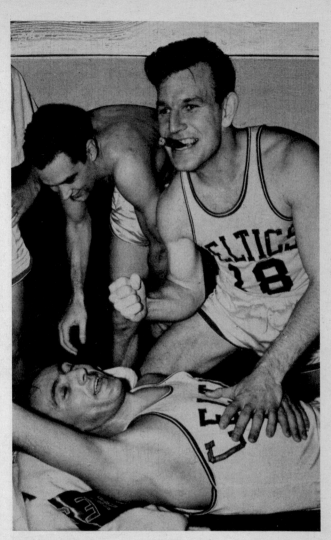

"Jungle Jim" Loscutoff smokes one of Arnold's victory cigars as he and Gene Conley try to revive me following a 1959 eastern divison playoff victory over Syracuse. (United Press International)

Bill Sharman is giving me a smooch after we won the NBA title from the Minneapolis Lakers in 1959. (UPI)

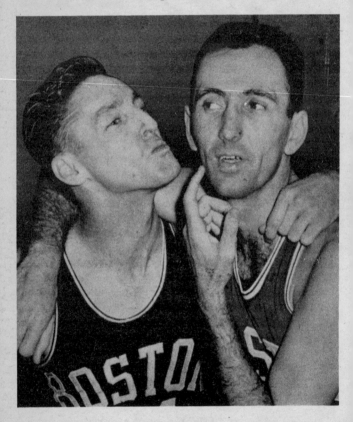

I'm driving down the middle against Philadelphia and Wilt, looking for help. (Bob Remer collection)

Arnold and I in a relaxed moment on the Celtic bench, 1961.

Arnold is addressing his troops after a long, hard practice session. Identifiable players, *left to right*, are Tom Sanders, Sam Jones, Bill Sharman, Bob Cousy, Frank Ramsey, Bill Russell, Tom Heinsohn, and K.C. Jones. (Russ Adams, *The Boston Herald*)

Arnold still has his coat on as we celebrate this 1962 NBA championship in the locker room. Tom Sanders is standing next to me. On Red's left are Sam Jones, Jim Loscutoff, and Carl Braun. (George Sullivan)

Back in the Garden in a 1963 game, I am pointing the way but seem to have left the ball behind for Tom Heinsohn. (Paul J. Maguire, *The Boston Globe*)

This hug was for a cystic fibrosis youngster at "Cousy Day" in 1963.

Russ can't believe I'm taking this shot.

My last season, the 1963 World Champion Boston Celtics. *Front row, left to right:* K.C. Jones, Bill Russell, President Walter A. Brown, Coach Red Auerbach, Treasurer Lou Pieri, Captain Bob Cousy, Sam Jones. *Standing, left to right:* Frank Ramsey, Gene Guarilia, Tom Sanders, Tom Heinsohn, Clyde Lovellette, John Havlíček, Jim Loscutoff, Dan Swartz, and Trainer Buddy LeRoux.

President Kennedy meeting our 1963 championship squad in the White House.

Are Russ and I singing a duet during our 1963 victory party? (Associated Press)

"Cousy Day," 1963, at a moment when the memories of thirteen great years really got to me. (Danny Goshtigian, *The Boston Globe*)

was putting together Public Service Announcements (PSAs) on racism. Would I mind introducing one or two? I said fine. I am not a crusader, but it happens to be a subject I feel strongly about. I don't mind being counted.

Then he called me the next day and said, "Would you mind doing another one on this trip?" I said, "You want me to do a couple, fine. Now you want me to do something in every city on this trip. I don't want to be a spoiler, but enough is enough." He calls me back the next day. He said he would give me $1,000. So now I am exploiting the situation if I accept. So now I suppose the purist would say, "Oh, you feel strongly about the racial issue, but you won't do the spot unless you get paid."

If you're in the public eye, you go through all sorts of mental contortions. You can only hope you're prepared for all this. Not many are these days. Every jock has a massive impact in this society, whether he or she likes it or not. What was true in the relatively innocent days of the '50s is even truer today, in this era of *People* magazine, "60 Minutes," and feature reporters on every sports staff in America.

Players are not given the moral foundation to act properly if the entire process begins with a sordid recruiting process. As he enters the professional ranks and comes to understand the cold-blooded nature of sports, he digs in. People want the image of a big happy family perpetuated, but both players and management know better.

Agents create hardened attitudes. By the time a kid signs a contract, what should be an exciting, healthy, and enthusiastic situation is already neutralized by the agent. The thought is instilled as soon as the kid signs the first contract, "OK, and if you have a good year, we'll beat them over the head." Common greed has immediately created an unhealthy atmosphere. The player looks at management and says, "What have you done for me lately?" This thought existed in the '50s, but not to the extent it does today.

The signals from management do nothing to erase the idea that anything goes. The big laugh in the NBA is the injury list. As soon as a team has a roster crunch, some player is designated to come up with the flu or the great catch-all, the bad back. Isn't it funny how many backs start acting up at opportune times in club histories? If management makes a farce out of the rules, why should someone in management be surprised when a player is caught doing drugs?

The big corruptor in the final analysis is the money. The commercialization of the game has altered outlooks drastically. I was the highest-paid player on the Celtics and I was making $30,000. The difference between my salary and that of the rest of the team wasn't all that much. The biggest discrepancy might have been $20,000 or so.

In a very real sense, we were like an army platoon. We were all in this thing together. We shared common problems. The league was still young, and there was inherent unity between teammate and teammate, player and coach, and even player and management. I've mentioned how Walter Brown was comfortable enough with us to ask for a delay in our playoff payout. Today, forget it. This guy wants more than that guy. This guy has to be the highest-paid player on the team, or the highest-paid power forward in the league, and the money differences are substantial. Instead of players approaching things with common problems, everything is an individual problem. I must admit I admire the Lakers for winning a second straight championship, given all these factors. I had convinced myself that repeats were not possible in this climate.

I really feel that if you're management you're better

off being a perennial contender than grabbing the brass ring. You open up a Pandora's Box by reaching that goal of winning the Super Bowl, the Stanley Cup, the NBA championship, or the World Series.

I really believe this. If you are a perennial contender, it minimizes to a certain extent your problem with agents and players coming into renegotiate. You can say, "Sure you had a good year, but the team didn't win."

It's also not a bad way to stimulate competition. We might have been better off in the long run by not winning the championship as easily and as often as we did. It never seemed to help our gate much the next year. We had to· wait until the playoffs to draw the sellout crowds. It wasn't easy, really, but people thought it was. We might have been better off the other way. Keep the athletes chasing the carrot, and keep the fans interested. The fans like to see a competitive situation. If this isn't true, then why was one of the two best attendance years of the entire thirteen-year Russell era 1966–67, when the Celtics finished second and Philadelphia won sixty-eight games?

I learned a lot from coaching college basketball. I encountered interesting situations in which I was able to observe myself, as well as others, justify some interesting ends to accomplish various means.

Whatever I thought I knew about myself was amplified by both the college and professional coaching experiences. Although I say it's difficult now for me to relate to the need for absolute success, I did go at the tasks with a certain amount of drive. I am a practical animal. When it became necessary for me to devote time to academics in high school, I did so. In my first three years in high school I was a C-minus student. I played only a year and a half of high school ball, and suddenly somebody came up to me and said, "Hey, do you know you have a chance to go to college on a scholarship? All you have to do is get your marks up the last year." Well, hey, no, I *didn't* know that.

I had never considered college, really. I worked my ass off that last year and became a B-plus student, or whatever, and got accepted at Holy Cross—all in one year's time. That spirit continued throughout my college career. We were underdogs at Holy Cross, but we won the NCAA championship my first year. That created more pressure to do well, naturally, and we all overachieved for four years.

That drive and dedication continued for me through that period, and again when I joined the Celtics. Once I left the Celtics I knew that it all came down to dollars. What does it take to sustain a certain lifestyle? Unfortunately, I suppose, I have never been overly ambitious with regard to finances. I never wanted to float into Monaco on my yacht. My goals have always been very realistic. Even finishing up with the Celtics while making $30,000 a year was fine to sustain what I had. I knew that if I exploited my fame properly, I would be able to increase my earning potential.

I looked upon college coaching as a part-time responsibility. This was 1963, and the scope of college basketball was nowhere near what it is today. Basketball wasn't especially important at Boston College. The school had gone to the NCAA tournament only once, in the late fifties. They played one game and were bounced out. BC was, and is, a hockey school in the winter.

Thank goodness we got some pretty good players at Boston College. For six years we were able to function effectively with me being more or less a part-time coach. After a while, when I started to get into it, my feeling was that the school's commitment to basketball was itself part-time. I didn't even have a full-time assistant.

So, I asked myself, am I going to put myself into an early grave to bring fame and glory to BC?

I had also matured to a point where I wasn't going to devote every waking hour to turning BC around, so to speak. When I made my decision to leave, I knew I could earn enough income outside of coaching. It wasn't a life-or-death situation.

That was twenty to twenty-five years ago. The pressure that is imposed today on these coaches at both the college and professional level requires complete dedication, and will cause burnout of the individual much quicker than in the past. You are not going to see the dear old kindly coach being retired forty-five years later by his alma mater. You are going to have more of what you've got today, especially in the colleges. There is constant turnover and complete breakdown in honoring contracts. How can you expect pro players to know how to act when they've watched their college coach walk out of a valid contract to seek greener pastures? The coaches don't have any apparent concern for the contracts, and in most cases the schools meekly acquiesce. It should be said, however, that schools share the same philosophy: What have you done for us lately? Win quickly or be gone.

Thirty or forty years used to be a long tenure for college coaches. Then it was twenty years. Now, it's a big deal if anyone reaches double figures at one school. It's different in the pros. Auerbach has talked for years about cycles and how they're getting shorter for teams. Once upon a time, a group was a group for six or eight years. Now it's down to three or four years, and there comes a time in most organizations when the players tune the coach out and a new voice must be brought in. That's hardly the case in college, where the players automatically turn over every four years, or five, with redshirted kids.

I think you'll not only continue to see coaches staying shorter and shorter periods at specific institutions, but that you'll also see coaches remaining coaches for shorter and shorter periods of time. At neither BC nor in the NBA did I ever dream of the full-time, eighteen hour-a-day commitment to coaching that seems to be necessary for success today. I'm not saying I don't respect it, but there is no way I could ever make that kind of commitment. If I didn't have so much on the griddle in other areas, maybe I would have. And there is simply more to this short life. Teaching people to play a child's game shouldn't have that high a priority.

But coaching has never been my complete bag. I've never been lazy in terms of my responsibilities, but I've always been highly expedient. The requirements for coaches are enormous. If you are beating the bushes fourteen hours a day and you are doing everything else that is required to put players on your collegiate roster, you might be able to turn your program around. But, under the current pressures you're almost guaranteed to burn yourself out.

One thing that has always mystified me is how college coaches can abrogate their basic responsibility to the kids, which is to get them educated. If you're going to go through the entire recruiting process and get the kid in school—for your purposes or for his—you have the further responsibility to see that the young man graduates. But that's the scandal. That, plus redshirting.

On that one I give myself the complete benefit of the doubt. We never redshirted anyone at Boston College. We really only had two opportunities I would have sanctioned. I said to the players, "It's your decision. It's a year out of *your* life, an additional year. I'm not going to tell you to take a year out of your life."

When I was coaching, redshirting was still newsworthy. It's built into football now. At the Division I level, with the exception of Notre Dame and the service academies (the conspicuous exception being Napoleon McCallum), the odds are well in favor of a player staying five years. There may be more justification now because of what is out there for them in terms of professional opportunities. An extra year will give a kid visibility and exposure, so he's doing it for himself as well as for the school.

Redshirting is done to bolster team depth. You tell me how many fifth year seniors are on the big name college teams, and we can construct the preseason Top Twenty. You need fifth year players in football, and more and more teams need junior college transfers in basketball. It's all part of the modern game. If an athlete understands the complete ramifications, even if a guy just wants another year of rah-rah and impressing the girls, I suppose that is fine, as long as it's his decision.

Every boy I recruited in my six years at BC received his degree. We were very proud of that. We felt it was a primary responsibility. Every two weeks or so we'd call the guidance counselors and find out which of our players was in trouble academically. There was a pragmatic side, too. We couldn't afford to lose anybody. I was doing it for them, and I was doing it for myself. We weren't like Ray Mears, with his 12 point guards. He must have had a helluva JV team.

Even then, you want to be careful how much you're doing for the kid, and how much he's doing for himself. Sooner or later he's got to learn to accept adult responsibilities and do things for himself. A lot of the products of *this* system are sent into the cold, cruel world without any idea what's going on.

Life for the sought-after jock is pretty soft. The least you owe that kid is a legitimate shot at a degree. The attitudes and maturity levels are sometimes shocking. At Cincinnati, we had Tiny Archibald, who emerged from four years at UTEP as a mute. And then there was Sam Lacey. Once, I fined him $500 for being overweight. Next thing I knew, he came in with $500 and said, "Okay, now I can eat." He thought that was all there was to it. So many players have no sense of responsibility. They get through their pro experience and they can't even mail a Federal Express letter. They have millions of dollars, but they can't function in society.

You think I'm kidding? Players don't have to buy airline tickets. They never have to stand in line for a flight: They are preboarded. They don't have to learn to figure a cab tip. When I played, buses were rare. You got into a cab, or if you could walk to the arena, you walked. Now whatever service the team doesn't provide, the player's agent does. What does a player have to do but show up for the game?

Unless players are totally mismanaged, they should leave the game today with a lot of money. When I quit, I was making $30,000, plus a few endorsements. Whatever money I have been able to put away has been because of my basic survival instincts. I have tried to be careful how I have exploited my name, and I have chased down just about every opportunity. But, I was the number one guy for a long time. What about the others? What about the Sweetwater Cliftons driving cabs in Chicago? There are many cases like that. Not every kid who makes the league sticks around very long. What else are they prepared for besides basketball?

It must be terrifying for kids who get cut when they know they're not prepared to do anything else. Remember that it's a racist society, and the odds are stacked against these black kids when they can no longer play.

A college kid has to figure out his approach. A lot of motives are self-serving. I remember Al McGuire saying he had looked into Jim Chones's ice box and noticed that Chones's wasn't as well-stocked as his.

Ice box—a beautiful choice of words. Those of us who have spent some time in the ghetto may not have known what a refrigerator was, but we sure could relate to that old "ice box." If you're a college basketball fan I'm sure you've noticed that having a way with words coupled with good solid street smarts and an Irish wit has worked very well for my old buddy Al McGuire. Some people accuse Al of being a faker, but it's just a question of using his talent and street experience to his advantage. Those of us who grew up in the streets of New York in the '30s and '40s can relate to that. Survival is still our primary instinct.

Dean Smith is probably the most universally re-spected coach in the business. His method requires dis-cipline and structure, but it's applied in a humanistic way. He's also bright enough to get full advantage from a situation and salvage whatever he can from the po-tential loss of a superstar—J.R. Reid, for example. Not always but in most cases it's in the young man's best interest to go to the pros early and "pack in" to today's market and lifetime financial security. The alternative is to stay in college for an additional year or two of eligibility and gamble that there will be no injury lead-ing to the loss of the once-in-a-lifetime opportunity in the NBA. The other side of this coin is the massive amount of time and effort that you and your staff have invested in recruiting the boy initially and the destruc-tive impact of his being lost to your program. What do you do if you're smart? You make the best of a negative situation. This is what Dean Smith and Al McGuire be-fore him have done. Wish the boy well and show the world that you have his best interests at heart. Chances are that you are not going to change his mind anyway, and by sending him off with a smile you immediately create a bond of credibility with every agent and ghetto kid you might be trying to recruit in the future. What the hell. Good politics and sensitivity to P.R. are part of coaching, too.

The bottom line on Bobby Knight is simply that he is bold, aggressive, creative, and innovative regarding his coaching techniques. His strongest asset may be the fact that he has never been insecure or reluctant to make changes. This was true even before he established an identity in his field. So many coaches are constantly looking over their shoulders. They restrict their talent and productivity because they're afraid to do something different. They take the safe path. They go strictly by the book. Not Bobby Knight.

Of course, on the other side of that coin are the coaches who allow their egos to overcome their good sense and their instincts. They constantly interject themselves into situations when the best move is no move—let the boys just play. If you've prepared them properly, letting them follow their instincts on the floor is probably best. This is especially true if you have the better team. Knight strikes a good balance between control of his teams and allowing them the freedom to play.

He engenders great loyalty from players who are not superstars, those without major talent but with a solid work ethic. They are less sensitive to criticism and in fact probably prefer to be coached by a hardliner who abuses them from time to time. This hardline approach doesn't work with the most talented or sensitive players, and those are the ones Knight has lost with his abrasive and immature style.

It's been said that when you're leading men you must treat everyone the same. In today's sports environment, in my judgment, given the spoiled, pampered athletes we are producing, the leader must be prepared to treat everyone differently. This is a tricky balance to maintain if you have an ego problem. It's also difficult to achieve without compromising the coach–player relationship. But it can be done if you're bright and sensitive to what's required and your ego does not demand the constant reassurance that you're the chief and they're the Indians: Do it my way, you son of a bitch, or else. Use the big stick when necessary, but don't be ashamed or embarrassed to employ the velvet touch when appropriate. I'm not certain Bobby Knight understands this need for flexibility.

If you're looking for a coach who is always going to get the most out of the talent he has to work with and by virtue of his knowledge and application, along with his dogged determination and a finely tuned competitive spirit, will always produce a successful and productive program, Knight is your man. You must be prepared to put up with his idiosyncrasies and his ego and hope that he matures, but what the hell, the last perfect man was crucified.

I go back a long, long way with Bob Knight, to when he was a twenty-four year old kid coaching at West Point. My first encounter with him might amuse people who have had run-ins with him.

Boston College accepted an invitation to scrimmage at West Point. I didn't know a thing about Knight as a player. I still don't. He was a fifth or sixth man at Ohio State when they had Jerry Lucas and John Havlicek. He was just this very young kid who for some reason has been handed the team at West Point.

Knight had some good players, including Mike Silliman, who played for the Olympic team and who would later be a member of the Knicks' 1970 championship team. He was a 6'6" forward who could do a lot of things.

We started scrimmaging, and within ten minutes it

was mayhem. We couldn't get anything done. "This isn't going to accomplish anything," I said. "This is the way we do it," was Knight's reply. We went back to the huddle. I remember saying to my guys, "Scratch this one. Just protect yourself. Do whatever you have to do."

For the next hour and a half all we did was break up fights. It was completely useléss. I remember saying, "This is the last time you'll see us, pal." Knight's philosophy had the perfect setting at West Point. He had all the structure and discipline he'd ever need. He could make killers out of those West Point cadets.

We wound up playing them for real that season in the Holiday Festival in Madison Square Garden. They were favored to win. We won the game in an upset. Knight had all that Army brass sitting behind him, and he kicked over the entire bench onto them. I went over, but Knight ran by me to attack the officials at midcourt. I wasn't going to wait for him to come back. I took off. We still hadn't shaken hands. I suppose I could relate to that. He was so pissed off he had to go after the officials. So big deal. He wouldn't shake hands.

Ours was the first game of a doubleheader. During the second game, I ran into Jack Donohue, the Holy Cross coach. He had Bobby Knight up against the wall. I just walked by. I don't know whether or not Knight saw me because he didn't say anything. A little later on I ran into Jack. "Jack, what was that all about?" I asked. He said, "You won't believe this." Tates Locke (who was Knight's predecessor at West Point, and helped him land the job) had called Jack during the week and said, "Are you doing anything Saturday night?" Donohue said, no, he wasn't. "Well," said Tates, "would you do me a favor? Would you go to New York and be a guardian angel? I am afraid of what Bobby might do if he loses to Cousy." Can you imagine that? He anticipated Knight's reaction.

That's the early Bob Knight, and in fairness to him, I don't think he has ever grown up. He acted like a spoiled McEnroe twenty-five years ago, and now, given his success, he should be able to keep his competitive instincts in line. A sore loser is bad, now and always. I should know. It always killed me to go over and shake the guy's hand after a game, when what I really felt like doing was kicking him in the groin. I was even a sore winner. I'd tell my players at BC, "Yeah, we won, but we didn't win *right*." If you're going to be successful, you've got to be a purist. The end result is fine. That's what it's about. But if the victory was accomplished in a sloppy way, I was upset. Knight carries this to an extreme.

I went through it myself, but I don't relate to dehumanizing players. I can't relate to Knight's ego, to the fact that he must be constantly catered to. I certainly don't relate to his excesses. He is a classic creature of this society.

Look at the effect he has had on the state of Indiana. He has produced three NCAA championships. Because he has been able to do this, he has intimidated everyone, starting with the former university president. He was allowed to get away with every form of intimidation and was allowed to control every aspect of his life. You could argue that Knight has simply made complete use of the tools he has had. If he knows that he can win by intimidating officials, he does so.

Knight doesn't care what you think or what I think. His big defense is always, "I graduate kids, and that's it." They graduate if they stay, that is. He's got a transfer rate rivaling the daily influx of illegals from below the border. Rick Calloway was good enough to start for him when he won the championship in 1987. A year later, Calloway transferred with one season of eligibility remaining. Interesting.

All Bobby has to do is mature. I look at things so

much differently now. I used to rationalize that it is a win-at-all-costs society and that to achieve victory the end justifies the means, but that's not properly preparing kids. In the end, it really *is* how you play the game, not whether you win or lose. Knight preaches this incessantly, but he constantly sends out the opposite message. There are no mixed signals in the state of Indiana, however. Do you think his bullying behavior would have been tolerated for ten seconds if he didn't produce the requisite number of victories? My whole life for a long time was dedicated to winning at any cost, but I no longer believe that. In terms of young people, at least, we have got to establish guidelines and rules.

That Holiday Festival game wasn't our last encounter at Boston College with Robert Knight. In 1969, we wound up playing them in the semifinals of the NIT. He had another excellent team, but we had a good one, too, and we were favored. We had won eighteen straight games after I had announced my retirement as coach.

In the game we fell behind by seven in the second half, which was like being down by twenty-five to anyone else, given the deliberate style Knight employed those days at West Point. But we played a spectacular second half, shooting something like sixteen for twenty from the floor. We got a basket that wrapped up the game with about two minutes to go. For the first time in the game, I sat back and relaxed.

We were able to strangle Knight's team at their own game. This win was a great achievement because Knight definitely had a good ball club. The only reason they hadn't gone to the NCAA, rather than the NIT, was Knight's refusal to miss the classroom time the NCAA would have required if the team had been successful. And they very well might have been successful.

While I savored the victory, I suddenly became aware of the sound of obscenities flowing by me. They were coming from my assistant, Gerry Friel, a pink-cheeked twenty-four year old who I had never heard utter a nasty word. Unbeknownst to me, Gerry and Knight had gotten into it at midcourt while the game was going on. I could hardly believe what was happening. Here we were, two minutes away from this big victory that would put us in the NIT finals, and my assistant and Knight were screaming obscenities at each other. As the game ended, the two had to be separated.

Again, I waited for the customary handshake, but we never got to that. Instead, Knight and Gerry went at it again. So Knight and I have never had a really meaningful conversation, despite playing each other twice, plus the scrimmage which kicked everything off.

I can relate to a lot of the forces that have governed Bob Knight. I've done a lot of stupid things in the name of competition, including kicking one poor guy in the head while going for a loose ball in a three-on-three game. In a meaningless tennis game, I can go through this Jekyll and Hyde transformation where I can't believe I do some of the things I do. It's all in the heat of the battle, so to speak. A lot of times, I wind up ashamed of the things I've done, but that is the killer instinct. That's the basic competitive instinct that's in me. But somewhere, at some point, you've got to draw the line, and a distinction has got to be made between what's right and wrong.

If Knight wants to be a sore loser, fine. I'm a sore loser. If he wants to kick chairs over, well, I remember when I punched a blackboard in New Orleans. You've got to release frustration sometimes. I can relate to all that. The point is, you do these things, and you are ashamed. Bob Knight, who is closer to fifty years old than to forty, has apparently not yet reached that stage.

Do you recall the incident in 1987 when he pulled

his team off the floor against the Soviets to protest the officiating? Keep in mind that he was about twenty points down at the time. That was no noble act. He wasn't forfeiting the game when he was ahead. Anyway, at his press conference afterward, he said, "Anybody out there who is without sin, let him cast the first stone." As if this were his first mistake. Amazing.

I would never think of publicly humiliating a player. Knight has had so many people leave his program. I remember one key guy—a captain, I believe. Supposedly, Knight had straddled him and called him all those four-letter words. Said he lacked courage and all that stuff. How do you use this as a learning tool? I am told on good authority that as harsh as the things were in the book about him that he detests, "A Season On The Brink," it was much worse before an editor stepped in. Some of the things he said to Darryl Thomas that year were vile.

To a point, I can relate this to Knight's competitive spirit, the fact that he is a basic sore loser, but, going deeper, maybe he needs psychiatric help. Why publicly humiliate kids? What is the good of humiliating your captain in front of his teammates when he is going to have to inspire them? To me, that seems just plain stupid and counterproductive.

You come to the point where you say, "That's just the way he is." He is somewhat predictable. Auerbach used to scream at us in general terms, but, Jesus, he was smart enough to know what my personality was like, and that I would have taken immediate personal offense if he had screamed at me, and me alone, in front of the other guys. He would have lost me. What good does that do you or the team?

Several of the Indiana players have survived the program and functioned well. Now they're held up as evidence that a good, tough kid can flourish and benefit from the treatment. Quinn Buckner is a good example. Bob Knight has nothing but good things to say about him. He brings Quinn back like a conquering hero. A lot of them swear that Bob is great. It is like boot camp. You are proud you have been through the experience. It's a macho experience you can tell all your friends about, and you're a tough man if you can survive it. But for those who can't stand to be humiliated, it is a stupid approach.

And what does it all come down to? It comes down to a kid making a very tough shot. If a guy made a free throw at the other end, and Knight's kid hadn't invented a winning basket at the offensive end, Syracuse would have won the 1987 NCAA championship and Indiana would have been a runnerup. Bob Knight had no control over either event. But now he can say, "Look at what my system accomplished." That's fine. But who thinks of the players who couldn't put up with Knight's system and dropped along the wayside?

The people who make the judgments are the people running the school. The citizens of Indiana, by and large, appear to be satisfied with the results. So Bob Knight can say to the rest of us, as he does, "I don't care about you." The school has got great alumni support, so who's going to curb him? Whatever he does, Knight can get away with.

Some of the things that happen to him are the result of provocations. But if you possess true adult maturity, you learn to walk away. That's a pretty easy case to make, whatever his style. It's a highly competitive society, and he's been very successful. He's a product of it. He has overcome, he has survived, and he has done very well. But now it's time to grow up, and he hasn't grown up.

I don't think there is a good reason for the continuance of all this. I assume Woody Hayes had the same complex. He ended up punching a kid while he was in his 60s, and he had to leave his job in humiliation.

However many friends Bob Knight has left are all afraid the end is going to be similar for him, that it will all come crashing down in some sort of Woody Hayes incident. People *do* care for him.

The incident with the Soviets bothered a great many influential people. He picked the wrong year to do a thing like that, I can tell you, because it coincided with his nomination for the Basketball Hall of Fame. He was still trying to live down the incident with the Puerto Rican policeman at the 1979 Pan-Am Games in San Juan, and then he pulled his team off the floor against the Soviets.

He wound up missing election to the Hall by three votes. To Europeans he is probably the premier name in coaching today, but I know people who said, "He may deserve it, but after the Russian embarrassment I'm not going to vote for him." He looked so incredibly foolish against the Soviets, picking up his marbles and going home when he was trailing by twenty. Maybe that, to some degree, is Knight's Woody Hayes incident. But you've got to wonder. At the end of that same season he threatened to leave for the University of New Mexico. I think he found out what he wanted to know, which was that every important person involved was willing to grovel to keep him. Once again, the school has endorsed him and told him, in effect, that he can do whatever he wants. It is a giant shame.

Knight's defenders say, "But at least he doesn't cheat." That's true. Bob has a lot of faults, but he doesn't cheat. Does this mean there is precious little in the middle-ground? That the only alternative to wholesale prostitution is to do it the way Bob Knight does? I certainly hope not.

*   *   *

Dealing with all the hypocrisy in college is enough to give you a headache. Coaching in the pros can give you an ulcer, but at least you're not operating under false pretenses.

I fell into professional coaching for one reason—the money. Sure, I had the pride factor going. It would have been nice to coach a champion, but the basic reason I allied myself with the fortunes of the Cincinnati Royals was the fact that I was being made the highest paid coach in NBA history at $100,000 a year for three years. This was 1969, and that was a lot of money.

— 10 —

The Up-Tempo Game

My approach as a college coach was to implement the "Celtic Mystique," a basic approach to how the game should be played. I was brought up on the running game, and that's what I wanted to teach to the eighteen and nineteen year olds I had at Boston College. I'm certain that any future ex-Lakers who go into coaching will try to carry on the "Lakers Mystique" because the basic underpinning of the L.A. approach in the eighties is no different than ours was in the fifties. Arnold picked up his fast break ideas from Bill Reinhart, *his* college coach at George Washington University almost 50 years ago. If an idea is good, it's good.

I entered college coaching without a lot of tutoring. I completed my professional career in May, and on the following October fifteenth I said hello to my first college team. What I did was purely from seat-of-the-pants instinct. I could implement the Celtics' principles, but I had to learn something about organization. That first year I felt we underachieved—we were 10–11—but that was primarily my fault because I did not prepare the team.

I engaged in a lot of wasted motion during my first year because I didn't know what I was doing. I spent a lot of time on little things instead of staking out my priorities in terms of what was required to win and keying on them.

Finally, I sat down and decided, "What the hell, we're going to run an up-tempo game." Our strengths and weaknesses dictated that approach and that was clearly the best way for us to win. From the first practice, we simply spent seventy percent of our time keying on the high priority items and a little bit of time on the other things. That's when we started working every day with our big inside people twenty minutes before practice. In the second year, we turned it around.

When I recruited players, I wanted to see a kid myself, in person. If I couldn't, I entrusted that responsibility to Frank Power, whom I trusted implicitly. They may be able to scout football players on film, with eight assistants sitting in the film room. They claim they can tell how quickly a running back hits the hole, and things like that. Well, I don't think it works the same way in basketball. I'd be very apprehensive about doing it in either sport.

From my second year at BC on, I was never an X and O man. What helped us establish ourselves was implementation of a double stack offense I picked up from Dee Rowe, who was then coaching at Worcester Academy. (Dee later went on to coach at the University of Connecticut.) The double stack worked equally well against zone and man-to-man defenses. It kept the ball in the hands of my best ballhandler, and I was fortunate enough during my time at BC to recruit excellent ballhandlers like Jack Kvancz, Billy Evans, and Jimmy O'Brien. The double stack was also a good vehicle for rebounding because it kept the big people where they belonged—inside.

My approach to the fast break was to minimize the

margin of error. You strived toward having every player do what he did best. The rebounder works, concentrating on boxing off. And when that big man gets the ball, he never, ever puts it to the floor. People used to kid me because day after day they'd hear me harping on the big players not to dribble. I was obsessed with it because I couldn't think of anything more frustrating than a big guy working to get the rebound only to hand it right back to the opposition for a layup because of sloppy ballhandling.

I drilled my big people on outlet passing. They were taught to look for the ballhandler, to make sure that after all their hard work the basketball was delivered to the right man. Sure it sounds elementary, but if you watch enough basketball at any level, you'll note how often big men get the rebound and have no clear idea of what to do next.

The next goal was to advance the ball with as few passes as possible. If you can get it upcourt with two passes rather than three, that was very good. That appealed to my conservative nature. Again, I was blessed with smart guards. Before Evans came along, I had a veteran named Ed Hockenbury. He wasn't very quick. He was built more like a football linebacker than a basketball player, but he was very smart and sure-handed. He knew how to run a team. When Evans and O'Brien came along, the tempo picked up. They had beautiful instincts on the break, and if we got the ball in the halfcourt and never ran a play, that was fine.

The voice of Auerbach was in the back of my brain. We talked about the Celtics having only seven plays. The idea was to get the job done with the least amount of wasted motion, reducing your margin for error. Arnold just wanted the pass to get there, which is why he had such a problem with my style in the beginning. "Just make the pass, damnit!" he would yell. If the behind-the-back pass got the job done, fine. If not, he would suggest forcefully that I forget the "fucking behind-the-back pass."

Today, players shoot the ball better than we did, but they don't really dribble it, pass it, or "think it," better. They've got all this talent, and they're coming up, some of them, with eighteen or twenty turnovers a game. I can't imagine having 20 turnovers a game in the old days! Coaches would say, "How can you beat *anybody* doing that?" A single turnover or two would have driven my old high school coach right up the wall.

Of course, you don't want to get obsessed with turnovers. Concerned, yes. Obsessed, no. I smiled this past year when I saw a clip of Temple coach John Chaney after a game against Villanova. Temple had one turnover in the second half, and Chaney kidded his players. "A turnover? A turnover! What happened?" Chaney is a real bug on avoiding turnovers. I admire his ability to get even three modern college kids, let alone eight or ten, thinking that way about turnovers. You just want to be careful not to have it all backfire by making kids gun-shy. You don't want to inhibit talent. Creative players like Larry Bird ought to have a turnover or two once in a while. All too often, a blank in the turnover column means a player hasn't been trying to create *anything*.

I guess you think this is funny, coming from Cous, Mr. Behind-the-Back. I'm associated with this behind-the-back stuff, even 25 years after I retired. Believe me, that was ten percent of my game. The other ninety percent was very conservative. I played that way and I coached that way. I picked my spots for the fancy stuff. Very simply, if the defense forces you to use an unorthodox move and you're physically capable of executing it even if the game is on the line, use it. Don't abuse it, however, or overuse it. I wanted to make very certain I could execute a trick pass if the game were on the line. Although you'd be far more likely to see me use one in a blowout. But the opposition never knew exactly what to expect, which was part of the psychology.

Ninety percent of the time I used bread-and-butter stuff. I would step in on the pass, the way they teach you to at basketball camp or in high school practice.

You've got to be wary of falling in love with the flashy stuff. The Celtics fell prey to it last year. Dennis Johnson had become very successful hitting Bird underneath with a bullet baseball pass from out on top of the key. Bird would either go back door on someone or get a baseline pick, and DJ would thread the needle with a real crowd-pleasing pass. There were stretches where they could be counted on for one of those collaborations each game.

It worked for a good deal of the 1986–87 season, but last season Johnson started to throw some of these passes away. Either they'd hit the backboard or they'd be batted away by a defender. The problem was that Johnson had gotten so cocky, he was throwing that pass from longer and longer distances. As he stepped over mid-court, I could see him looking for Bird. He was making the pass without any apparent concern about the length of it or the positioning of the defense.

I saw both Bird and Ainge becoming careless last year, especially on the road. When you allow a little of that, it becomes a snowball heading straight downhill. Pretty soon five guys are being careless. This is how a team that had been a great road team for a couple of years slowly becomes a very ordinary team away from home. The Celtics were not paying attention to detail, and they were no longer inherently powerful enough to dispatch people just by showing up.

Problems ensue when you stop "thinking" the game.

Hell, we all take the path of least resistance. Watching players come through the system we have today—both the high schools and the colleges—I guess I shouldn't be surprised by what I see.

Anyway, once we committed to the up-tempo game at Boston College and established that as the cornerstone of our philosophy, we were ready to do some damage. We were scoring in the nineties and the hundreds. We were having fun. Fans were being entertained. And we were winning games. We beat Rhode Island in a great game, 107–105. We beat Utah State and the late, great Wayne Estes in the Rainbow Festival by a 120–118 score in overtime. Estes scored fifty-two. Our John Austin had forty-two. We won the game on a jump shot by our captain, George Humann.

An up-tempo game benefits everyone. It makes the nonshooters shooters and it makes the shooters better shooters. During my last season, a BC player named Tom Verroneau shot sixty-five percent for the season, and he had about a three-foot range. He cleaned up as the finisher on the break and as a basic garbage man. His personal success demonstrated clearly how well an up-tempo game gets everyone involved. In some ways Kurt Rambis was the Tom Verroneau of the Lakers. He's not what they call a "go-to guy," but he has had a consistently high shooting percentage as a Laker because he has functioned as a part of their up-tempo whole.

When big men with moderate or even very limited offensive talent know that the frequency of reward is great, they work harder. Rather than being put down for their limited scoring abilities, as they would be in a strict halfcourt offense, they eagerly participate in the rebounding. If you are playing a controlled offense, the big men do the dirty work, the defensive rebounding and the hard defense at one end, and then set picks at the other end. The only time a big man gets a shot in a controlled offense is if he rebounds offensively, which is just about the hardest job of all.

Obviously, this wears a guy down mentally, because *everybody* thinks he is a shooter. But an up-tempo game gets everyone involved. It creates more enthusiasm and motivation to work on defense and then run down the floor. It's mandatory, of course, that your point guard understand all this and recognize his responsibility to get the ball to the big guys.

Playing up-tempo basketball improves your whole shooting posture and improves your mental approach to the offensive game. It puts constant pressure on the defense, and it neutralizes a lot of pressure you might normally get. The last three or four years I coached at BC, we hardly saw any defensive pressure. The last time we saw really good defensive pressure was in 1964 when UCLA pressed us in a Christmas tournament in Milwaukee. They had the guys who could play that kind of game.

But after that I'm sure other coaches were saying, "Boston College is going to run at every opportunity." We wanted to control those opportunities. The only time we faced pressure was late in games, under predictable circumstances. Another advantage of our style was that we never had overpowering big people. The biggest player I ever had was 6'10", and he didn't play much. Our big people topped off at 6'8", and this lack of size minimized the offensive board pressure our front line had to face. In college you can't tell a player, "Hey, get the best shot, but get back on defense." People didn't crash the boards on us very much because they respected our quick-strike capability. This was especially true when we had Terry Driscoll, who, though just 6'7", was one of the truly great practitioners of pivot play in the history of college basketball.

Driscoll was a superior rebounder, and he could throw the outlet pass right up there in the class with Bill Russell, Wes Unseld, and Bill Walton. He had very large hands, and he could rifle the ball on a line just about the length of the court. I'll never forget a night against Duquesne in the Pittsburgh Civic Center. It was as if they had never scouted us because they kept sending their big men to the boards for second shots, rather than concentrating on getting back on defense. Duquesne had the Nelson twins, who stood 6'10", and 6'8", but none of their big men could beat Driscoll to the ball. As a result, we spent the entire first half executing a layup drill. They caught on in the second half, but we won the game by twenty.

Right now, people are asking how the Celtics can restore their running philosophy when they don't appear to have very good overall team speed. While it's true that nobody is going to come up with a magic compound to rub on Larry Bird's legs to make him as fast as James Worthy, it's equally true that being a cheetah has very little to do with being a fast break basketball player.

There is no greater myth in basketball. I don't know how fast I was. I couldn't have beaten my grandmother down the court in a race. Obviously, it helps if your front court has good speed. The Lakers have benefitted from the exceptional speed of Worthy, A.C. Green, and Michael Cooper, when he's playing in the frontcourt. But to have blazing speed is not a prerequisite for a fast break offense.

Robert Parish isn't *that* fast, but he gets up and down the floor well. He responds to the moment. When he sees his opponent putting himself in a certain posture, Robert takes off. The important thing is that the team be well-drilled in the outlet pass. I was interested to see that Bird called for the reinstitution of the long-pass drill at daily practice, now that there has been a change in coach. He said the team had to "get back to basics" if it wanted to be the running team Jimmy Rodgers seeks. I couldn't agree more.

The outlet passes are the key and if you get the ball into the hands of your point guard, the issue is how quickly he gets it from the top of your key to the top of the opposite key. How far is that? Only about sixty feet, no more. You've got to get five guys to cover that distance as quickly as they can by establishing the proper mind set. There are five or six ways you can create a breaking situation—missed shots, missed free throws, steals, among them—and you need five guys to respond *automatically*. It's all in the timing, and of course the desire. The court is ninety-four feet long. The point guard and the off guard are only covering fifty or sixty feet.

The inherent advantage the offense has is that even if a player on the defense knows a fast break is coming, he is not going to be as enthusiastic getting back down the floor on defense as he is heading up on offense. You have all these factors working in your favor if the timing is right. Speed is an asset, but it is not critical. After the rebound, the most important thing is the point guard getting the ball to the other key as quickly as possible and then making the pass that leads directly to the score. Ideally, you'll have two passes.

There are good technical role models for kids today, if they know where to look. I suggest they start in Los Angeles and Philadelphia.

How could I not like Magic Johnson? I don't know him, so I don't know whether he's responding to situations intellectually or instinctively. But he does things with the least amount of wasted motion, a quality I admire in any player. That's one thing he shares with Bird. Just get the job done. There is a time to show off and a time to do it the way you are supposed to. Bird and Magic understand the difference.

I don't see this quality as much as I'd like to in Isiah Thomas. He says he's learning the difference, and there were indications during the 1988 playoffs that Thomas has learned something. But I'm not sure if he has the message. When a team has got something going, the point guard is the one who at all costs has to keep the momentum going. If he does something stupid and doesn't accomplish his purpose, that has a horribly negative effect on the team. It will put the brakes on the whole flow.

Magic doesn't do this. He hits the outside shot more now, which I think he should because it's been there for him for years. The best percentage for opponents has been to give him the outside shot, if you've got to give him anything at all. Now he takes it more, and hits it more. Magic made the adjustment two years ago. Evidently, Pat Riley told him to be offensive minded, and he responded. Magic doesn't take bad shots. He never forces a play. He penetrates, and he's always looking to make the play. He understands the basic point man criterion: Every time you pass halfcourt your first thought has to be how to create an opportunity for someone else, not yourself. This is what Isiah was slow in learning. All too often, he came across midcourt looking to do his thing. If you understand the psychology of the position, and you realize that your basic job is to pass out the sugar to the other four guys, you can't be coming across thinking "shoot."

It doesn't take long for *this* old point guard to size up point guards. I can tell immediately what's in their minds. People tend to equate the job of point guard with being "unselfish." They assume that someone without an ego will have a better shot at being an effective point guard because he is willing to share the glory, as opposed to being in the limelight.

I don't buy that theory. I think it takes a specific personality to be a point guard, but it doesn't have anything to do with being unselfish. A point guard wraps up his identity in distributing the basketball. He is recognized for that skill. If he makes a good pass, he wants to see the play finished off properly. If it isn't, there won't be a basket, and he won't get an assist.

A point guard takes pride in creating an opportunity for someone else, but it's all in the context of helping the team win the game. He's got to understand at all times the impact, mentally and physically, of everything he does.

If basketball is an art form, as I think it is, and there are six, seven, or eight bodies moving quickly within a confined area you have to rely on your instincts to create an opportunity. When you get to the penetrating area you've got to realize that everything you now do is going to have an impact on the defense. I used to tell my point guards at Boston College these things all the time. The slightest movement—a little left shoulder dip—is going to take the pressure off the right side, so don't dip that shoulder if you have made up your mind you want to go to the right lane. A dribble here is going to force the defense to adjust, and whatever you do as long as you remain "alive" is going to have an impact on the defense.

This is where the thinking comes in. It *is* a selfish act in terms of wanting to be effective and knowing that what you do is going to be both useful to the team and entertaining for the fans. If I went through this and that only to see Dickie Hemrich blow the layup, he'd hear from me in no uncertain terms afterward. Here I create a beautiful play, I figure, the other guy should take pride enough to concentrate on making the layup.

You've always got to be thinking. I've already said that a point guard should cross midcourt thinking "pass." But he shouldn't come over thinking, "Okay, the big guy is in the right lane. I'm going to the right lane, so I'm going to dip my shoulder and that is going to open it up." You have to be prepared. If you are being guarded by a dummy, and he doesn't even go for the fake but hangs in there, you have got to be prepared to make an instant adjustment. You don't come across midcourt with a preconceived notion of what you're going to do because ultimately the defender, or the two defenders, are going to decide for you. Suppose they don't go for the fakes, and fall off in anticipation of a pass and you're not prepared to go into your shot option? You can't fall into the trap of thinking pass all the time. Then you will be far less effective. You have got to have a mix. You must have the ability to take it in yourself, which, of course, Isiah, Magic, Mo Cheeks, and all the good ones are able to do. You never concentrate on one option to the exclusion of the others. Thinking pass first means just that. It doesn't mean to think about passing exclusively. Think pass and shoot if you have to.

That was no misprint a few lines back. I lumped Mo Cheeks in with Magic and Isiah because I think he's in their class. In fact, Mo Cheeks is the prototypical point guard. If I were a coach, and I were talking to a bunch of young kids, I'd tell them that the Mo Cheeks way is the way a point guard should play the game. At the same time, if I have a choice of any player at that position today, I will go with the guy who is 6'9". Magic has the talent to create opportunities and the talent to go showtime. I think Magic, unlike his good buddy Isiah, has the basic instincts of *when* to go showtime and when to stay conservative. Magic has it all. Riley did a smart thing two years ago when he stopped playing mind games with Kareem and sold him the idea that the time had come to turn the keys over to Magic as leader of the team.

Magic is 6'9", which puts him in a totally different category. He has been the team's best rebounder for a number of years, another example of his tremendous versatility. He is more than a point guard. His value to the Lakers extends to many areas.

Maurice Cheeks is listed at 6'1". He's probably 6', tops. He has one job—point guard—and in the strictest sense of the job description I think he has been the preeminent point guard in the NBA for many years. You always look for examples for kids to emulate and not to emulate. Mo Cheeks just touches all the bases. He is a completely reliable point guard. More than any player in the league, he is truly the proverbial extension of his mentor's thinking while on the floor. Dave Wohl, who as an Ivy League graduate has a nice way with words, once said that Mo Cheeks was plugged into Billy Cunningham's neurons. I'm not sure how technically accurate that is, but it sounds about right to me.

Mo leads, he penetrates, and he doesn't throw the ball away. He lays it down to the right man when it is required, and he always makes the proper pass for the occasion. It may not often be spectacular, but he manages to get the job done with the least amount of wasted motion. And how many point guards give you his perpetually intense defense? None. He expertly plays the passing lanes. He is always in the top two, three, or four in steals. He's a master at double-teaming: He knows exactly when to risk leaving his man. He recovers very well. When he decides to gamble, most of the time his thinking and execution are so good you wouldn't call it a gamble.

At 6'1", Cheeks is not a rebounder, but he's a lot like

Norm Van Lier, who was just about the same size. The Bulls under Dick Motta had Tom Boerwinkle, who was 7′, Bob Love, who was 6′8″, Chet Walker, who was 6′6″, and Jerry Sloan, who was 6′6″. But guess who used to come down with the key rebounds for the Bulls? Norm Van Lier. Forgive me for waxing a bit nostalgic about Norm Van Lier. He started out with me in Cincinnati, and I loved him as a player. But it was tough going with two small guards in Van Lier and Tiny Archibald. We needed a big man, so against a lot of my emotions and better judgment I traded him to Chicago for a 6′10″ journeyman named Jim Fox. Jim did an okay job for us, but I must admit I always regretted trading Norm Van Lier. It was the worst move I ever made. He was an unbelievable hustler, and he had guts.

Cheeks is reminiscent of Norman in some ways. He responds to the moment, and he makes the play that has to be made. He has no visible weaknesses. Every part of his game is solid. People say, well, he has never scored very much. Thirteen per game is a big year. That's true. But there was a year not too long ago when of all the guards in the league Mo Cheeks had attempted the fewest shots per game of any player averaging twenty or more minutes a game. He has never been confused about what he's supposed to be doing out there.

Mo Cheeks can shoot. He may not have three-point range, but he's a very reliable middle distance shooter who invariably shoots fifty percent or more from the floor. He can get you twenty points any night he's left alone. He doesn't search out his own shot very often, that's all. Cheeks is a dangerous open shooter, but he never forces a shot. He just takes the ones that naturally turn up.

Penetration, however, is Cheeks's forte. This takes hard work, and Cheeks has never been afraid of that.

Cheeks's sense of what the team needs is uncanny.

He knows when the 76ers really need penetration to the basket, which is particularly important when the team has the imposing offensive presence of Charles Barkley in its midst. Cheeks knows that when you really need a hoop he can get by his man and make something happen for somebody. When you have that ability, you are going to create something positive for your team if you know how to exploit this talent. Mo Cheeks instinctively does this. Isiah Thomas doesn't, at least not that I can see.

Mo Cheeks does absolutely nothing on the floor that isn't geared to successfully execute the play. There is no fat whatsoever in his game. It's all meat. The professionals all respect him, but the average guy would never think of equating him with a Magic or an Isiah.

Cheeks is a victim of the times. Every NBA promo keys on players making a fancy dunk shot. People treat the annual Slam Dunk Contest at the All-Star Weekend as if it's meaningful. Guys sulking over the voting. Oh, brother. If those who elect the team had a common sense or sound thinking about competition, Maurice Cheeks would be elected. But the fans would rather canonize somebody who dribbles between his legs a hundred times a game than a good, smart player.

The big thing during the last ten years is being able to dribble between your legs for no other reason than to show the world you can do it. You'll see guys burned bringing the ball up after losing the ball in a needless dribble between their legs. It's all completely unnecessary. You're just bringing the ball upcourt. The basic concept is to get the ball upcourt as quickly and efficiently as possible. You don't see Mo Cheeks dribbling the ball between his legs without a purpose.

My opinion has nothing whatsoever to do with ego. I'm not going to give you any bull about playmakers being "unselfish." As a point guard, you bring a great deal of pride to what you do. Your role is to run the team and produce baskets. I love watching guys who can pass and who relish what they do. If you've got the talent to pass, you can turn me on. I don't assume you're being unselfish. I assume the opposite. I figure you like what you do, you're proud of your ability, and you get a charge out of seeing your hard work pay off in a basket. I figure you're like me. If the guy misses the shot, he's going to hear from you, the way the Celtics used to hear from me.

I'd like to think coaches out there are getting the message across to kids, pointing out the dos and don'ts and steering the young players with talent toward the right role models. I'd like to think that, but I rather doubt it. How many kids are sitting out there in the cities, from Boston to Seattle, looking at Maurice Cheeks, and saying, "There's *my* man"? Not too many. But if there were more players like Mo Cheeks around, the game would be much better. We'd all enjoy watching it more.

Who am I to talk? Back in the fifties and sixties I used to get letters all the time from high school coaches saying, "Will you stop with that behind-the-back pass? Do you know what damage it's doing to my kids?" As I've explained, ninety percent of my game was conservative. But that's not what the kids wanted to imitate. It's the same today. Kids aren't imitating Maurice Cheeks, and they aren't imitating the sound parts of Magic's game. They see a lookaway pass or, worse yet, a between-the-legs dribble, and that's what they try to imitate.

Mark Jackson of the Knicks is the latest rage. I'd like to see more of him. He was the Rookie of the Year last season, but I still have some reservations about him. He benefitted from the situation. Rick Pitino handed him the job immediately. I don't know that I would have turned loose a Gerald Henderson or a Rory Sparrow that quickly, but Pitino was new and he wanted to make a statement with his own people. He didn't want any carping veterans around, especially at point guard.

I'm not knocking Jackson. Basically, I like the way he plays. I think he has the right instincts. But the overall polish is yet to come. I'm not sure he has all the necessary conservative instincts to run in the show in the front court. There is more than a little hot dog in him, so he's got to be careful not to get caught up in the flashy stuff for its own sake. In New York that might not be an easy instinct to fight.

Another young point guard I think needs work is Kenny Smith of Sacramento. He seems to have a strong desire to get his fifteen shots a night. That's not a good idea in the first place, but I also don't think he is that good a shooter. Smith is also very skinny, and when he penetrates he is not exactly going to overpower anyone. If you've got no one else, you play him. It's like the Nets' John Bagley. You play him, because you *have* to play him. He may get the job done up to a point.

Bill Fitch (or somebody) came out with a great line about Bagley. With Bagley, you will allow to be deluded for a couple of games, a week, or even a month that he can do the job, but he *can't*. He is just competent enough to get the job done for a while if you have no one else. But Bagley is limited. If you strengthen other areas, you'll realize that Bags isn't good enough to get you over the top.

At Boston College, I once had two point guards of high quality in Billy Evans and Jimmy O'Brien, and I had them on the same team. A kid like Evans is an interesting study. He was the only white player on the Hillhouse High team in New Haven, Conn., and he was respected enough to be elected the team's captain. They were state champs, and their star player was a 6'5" moose named Walter Esdaile. Esdaile had a good head on his shoulders, and he went to Cornell. Evans wasn't highly sought after. For one thing, he wasn't much of a shooter.

We didn't have a giant recruiting battle. I don't think the high-powered folks in the Atlantic Coast Conference were after him. If they had been and they really wanted him, I would never have had a chance to recruit him. Evans turned out to be ideal for what I wanted to accomplish. Billy Evans was an extension of his coach on the floor. I believe there are always worthy kids like Evans out there. They are not the blue chippers, but they have intelligence and an obvious capacity for growth. A school that doesn't deal in blue chippers should be on the lookout for a smart kid that will be able to make progress through the program.

The NBA is no different. Mo Cheeks was a second round draft pick. Philly got him because Jack McMahon, an old adversary of mine (he played on those excellent St. Louis teams that formed our first big interconference rivalry), latched onto Mo and highly recommended him to the 76ers. Cheeks's story somewhat parallels that of Tiny Archibald. He was a city kid (DuSable High in Chicago) who escaped the attention of the Big Ten, the Big Eight, and other Bigs, and went to school in Texas, as Tiny did. In Mo's case, the school was West Texas State in Canyon, Tex., not too far from Amarillo. Like Tiny, Cheeks didn't score much. Unlike Tiny, he didn't possess explosiveness on offense. Tiny had to be shaped into being a true point guard. Mo's inclination for the position was much more natural.

But nothing changes. If now until the end of time owners or even coaches in the NBA have a choice between an Isiah Thomas and a Mo Cheeks, they are going to take Isiah. The more glamorous players will have the advantage.

This is why Magic is so special. Here is a truly glamorous player who can also get the job done. Five championships are testimony to that. Magic can make the distinction between fun and business. He knows when to put on the show to entertain the fans, and sell those tickets, and when to turn his attention to the business of winning the basketball game. If he were to put on his best show, but the team didn't win enough, there would be a question about his priorities. There is a balance to be met, and he has found it. The bottom line is that you go for the spectacular player first, hoping he can understand the necessary distinctions. As much as anyone ever has, Magic Johnson understands. Completely.

You must love Magic in the All-Star Game. He's the guy who keeps you in your seat. He does all the things you wouldn't want him to do in an important game. He gives you the lookaway pass, and the wraparound pass, the things that would drive his poor coach through the ceiling if the game were for real. But in that format, Magic's approach is ideal. They go out there to show off, have fun, and, hopefully, win the game at the same time. Winning is not the priority.

One thing Magic, Isiah, and Mo have in common: they are all up-tempo players. I wouldn't have minded having one of them at Boston College.

— 11 —

Up-Tempo and
Tiny Archibald

I FELL INTO professional coaching for one reason—the money. Sure, I had my pride going. It would have been nice to coach a champion, but the basic reason I allied myself with the fortunes of the Cincinnati Royals was the fact that I was being made the highest paid coach in NBA history at $100,000 a year for three years. This was 1969, and that was a lot of money.

I never entered college coaching with the idea of gravitating toward the NBA. I really didn't keep in close contact with the Celtics after my retirement. They were busy going about their business and I was busy going about mine.

The first time any discussion about professional coaching arose was about the time of Red's last year, 1965–66. Red had announced he would be quitting at the conclusion of that season, and Jack Waldron was representing the owners of the Celtics.

I had a meeting with Arnold and Jack where they broached the subject of me replacing Auerbach. The big hitch was that I had just signed a new three year contract at Boston College. I was seriously interested in coaching the Celtics, but I was young and naive. This was before the era when it was routine to renegotiate or skip out on contracts. I said, "Jesus, I'd love to coach the Celtics, but I have this new contract with BC." That didn't cut much ice with Waldron.

It really would have been uncomfortable for me, since I had already asked BC athletic director Bill Flynn to hold the job open for me during the final year of my playing career. Frank Power coached the team on an interim basis while they waited for me. How could I now go back to a man who was gracious enough to do a thing like that and say, "I'm sorry, but you've got to let me out of the contract." It's not as if I would have done Frank Power a favor, either. He was not interested in coaching full-time. His day job was in the Boston school system. He coached as an avocation, and he was doing Bill Flynn a big favor when he took over the team. In addition, at that time I was enjoying the experience at BC.

So that's when Red chose Russell to coach. And I have grave reservations about how it would have worked out between Russell and me, if I were the coach.

Three years later, the Royals contacted me about the job in Cincinnati. I went to Arnold and asked him what he thought about the whole thing. I figured he'd have a good read of the situation in Cincinnati. I knew very little about it, having spent the previous six years immersed in the college game.

To my surprise he said this was going to be Russ's last year. So why didn't I wait and he would hold the job open for me? There was one major problem, however. There was a $70,000 discrepancy between the $100,000 Cincinnati was offering and Red's offer. Now I was not above making a slight adjustment in my thinking for the chance to coach the Celtics, but I couldn't make that big a financial sacrifice. Obviously, I said thank you very much, and went to Cincinnati.

I didn't go into professional coaching highly motivated. When I left BC at the conclusion of the 1968–69 season, I made a commitment to get out of coaching. Oh, if an opportunity had arisen that was attractive to me on the college level to continue coaching, I think I would have continued to enjoy it. But I had no interest at all in coaching on the professional level. I never explored coaching in the pros because I enjoyed coaching on the college level. Even when Arnold asked me to coach the Celtics, I could have come up with a rationalization to take the job. It's like everything else in life. If there is something you want badly enough, I suppose you find ways to do it.

The Royals were a pretty grim situation. They had enjoyed a good run in the mid-sixties, but they were never good enough to beat the Celtics when it mattered. By the time I arrived, Oscar Robertson had been in the league for eight seasons and was dead set in his ways, which didn't include the topic nearest and dearest to my basketball heart: up-tempo basketball. Jerry Lucas was another experienced veteran star who did things his way. I realized quickly it wasn't going to work between us, and I traded both of them, searching for young talent.

A few die-hard basketball fans were upset about losing Robertson and Lucas, but most sports fans in Cincinnati didn't care much one way or the other. The truth is that the Royals didn't exactly have the town by the throat.

It was a negative situation, but I really didn't become completely *uncomfortable* until my final season. Initially, I looked on the job as a three-year responsibility. I could take that $300,000 and put it away. I was making income from other sources, and I didn't need the Royals' salary to live on. I was able to defer the whole thing. This was an important financial tactic for me because basketball had no pension plan at the time. I didn't have any savings to speak of. That being my whole purpose, there was very little motivation for me beyond the money. As a result, the situation never got much better.

I was reluctant enough, and I soon found that I didn't feel as comfortable with professionals as I had with college kids. Cincinnati was a conservative town, and we were playing in an old building that had no discernible charm. That first year we tried hard to promote the team. We did radio, television, the Kiwanis Club—the whole routine—and we got very few results. It didn't seem to have any impact on the size of the crowds, and trading Oscar and Lucas didn't help the gate any, either.

After three fruitless seasons in Cincinnati, during which time our peak victory total was thirty-six and we never made the playoffs, the franchise was moved to Kansas City (not to mention Omaha) for the 1972–73 season. The move to Kansas City brightened the situation a little because there was an opportunity to establish a franchise in a new city. We had the chance to create a good attitude in a new locale. The response at first was somewhat better, although I would never label it as "great." But you certainly felt there was a better chance of making it in Kansas City. The overall situation was more encouraging.

I hate to say it, but the four-plus years I spent coaching the Royals were wasted. I could have been back home in Worcester doing something productive. Of course, I wouldn't have been paid $100,000 a year doing anything else, either.

Nothing ever happened to get us excited. If we had gotten Dave Cowens in the 1970 draft instead of Sam Lacey, I probably would have stayed a few more years. In addition to being a great player, Cowens would have been a box office dream. He was born and raised in Newport, Ky., right across the Ohio River from Cincinnati. It's all one metropolitan locale: when you fly into Cincinnati, you land in Kentucky. Cowens was a big attraction when the Celtics came to town.

But we didn't get Dave Cowens, and in my heart I knew then what I acknowledge now. That job was a graveyard. Even if we had gotten Cowens, and won more games, would we ever have been good enough to get over the hump? By winning games we would have had lower draft choices, and we needed a lot of help.

What frightened me was my lack of control. The draft system is pure chance, even moreso now for the teams placed in the lottery. In a sense I threw in the towel too quickly, but on the other hand, I never would have felt that way in my college situation. I am a firm believer that in college, if you are not afraid to work and you have reasonable knowledge and talent, within three to five years you can have a competitive team. You have some control over your destiny.

The hopelessness of the situation in Cincinnati is what used to upset me more than anything else. The Lacey-Cowens juxtaposition was totally frustrating. We absolutely needed a center. My center the first year was Connie Dierking. We couldn't go one more year like that. I went to see Sam play three times that year. Each time I went to see him he got worse. I would walk out. I said, "We have *got* to get Cowens." Then we ended up where we did, and the Celtics got Cowens one pick ahead of us.

So I chose somebody I really didn't want and hoped he could function. It's not like college, where you live with the guy for three or four years. You might have to live with this guy for *ten* years. It really is a terrible situation. You can do all the work you want, spend lots of money on scouting, and gather together all your expertise, but when you come down to it, either you're lucky or you're not.

I guess for this reason I didn't give the Royals the full commitment. I could have worked harder and worried more about it. I started with a three year commitment, extended it to four, and eventually went to a fifth year before I realized I had made a serious mistake. I looked at it as a job I had to do. I had to put in my time and then get out. Maybe in that sense I shortchanged the responsibility, but if you haven't got the players, it just doesn't happen. Finally, I woke up one morning that fifth year and said, "What the hell am I doing here?" And I quit.

Kansas City was a graveyard situation. If I had nothing else going, I would have stayed there. I could still be coaching, I suppose. I figured we were going to be drafting in the middle of the pack for the foreseeable future, and the best we could hope for with that nucleus was making the playoffs.

My big policy decision was to make Tiny Archibald the focus to encourage him to be a superstar. It was like giving the kid the keys to the car and saying, "It's all yours," but it was our most expedient move. Tiny had the individual skills to create offense for himself and others simultaneously, as he proved when he became the first and only player to lead the NBA in both scoring and assists during the '72–'73 season, our first as the Kansas City–Omaha Kings. The other consideration, and it was a big one in our circumstance, was that he was entertaining. If there is one thing people can identify with in basketball, it's the little man. Watching a 6'1" guy do the things Tiny did, night after night, was a fabulous entertainment spectacle.

Tiny was so effective that we definitely won more

games with him than we would have won otherwise. He really frightened people. I remember coming into the Boston Garden. Tommy Heinsohn had the Celtics off to a 10–0 start. He was worried about Tiny, so he rigged a very thinly disguised zone defense to stop him. Tiny got thirty-five points and fifteen assists and we beat them. That's the year the Celtics won 68. Don't forget, one of those fourteen losses came to the Kansas City–Omaha Kings.

I knew very well that allowing Tiny to dominate the game completely was not the way to go for the future. It was, however, an easy way to go. It was in my head to leave after three years anyway. Then Joe Axelson, the general manager, talked me into staying a fourth year. Then I was thinking in terms of four years, before Axelson pressured me again. When I said I would stay another year, I knew I had made a mistake. My heart wasn't in it. It was easier for me to go along with his priorities rather than my own, and I paid for it.

The downside of encouraging Tiny Archibald to be the whole show was that I was doing nothing to enhance his ability as a point guard. The virtuoso act gave him a public identity, but it wasn't until he blended in with the Celtics for six years that he reached his fulfillment as a player and an athlete.

Tiny worked hard, and that was good because I wanted the team to be known for something. A team with thirty-five wins isn't going to excite anybody, so you've got to make sure they work hard enough to get people's attention. This is what I used to key on. I wanted to at least believe that Cousy's teams hustled.

I used to scream a lot at them. It was a constant battle to get my message across. I took it to an extreme during the final game of my second season. We were in the Boston Garden and we were getting our doors blown off. I suppose it was doubly frustrating for me because losing this way was bad enough but losing to a rejuvenated Celtics team (being led by Dave Cowens, the guy we wanted) was even worse. They had won their division and were on their way to the playoffs; we weren't going anywhere but home.

I used up all our timeouts by the middle of the third period and so, and once you do that you incur a technical foul if you call any more. I didn't care about that. I was furious with the team for the way they were playing, and I called as many timeouts as I wanted to deliver my orations. We weren't going to win that game if I could have used seven men at a time.

I tore in to them. I said, "We will be here until two in the morning. We are going to call timeouts until you get this." Basketball is an emotional game. No one is ever going to convince me otherwise.

You've got to do something to trigger responses in players. You do it too often, and they get bored. They will let down. You have to understand all these things, and then do what your personality tells you to do. In this case, even in the last game of the season, my personality told me to call those timeouts to make my point.

Sometimes you just can't avoid it. You've got to play the big, bad boss. I once even had to discipline Tiny, who was practically the whole team.

The same thing happened in college. The superstar violates a rule, and, boy, the other ten or twelve guys watch to see what happens. From a coaching standpoint you are on the spot. You are going to either alienate the star temporarily or lose your credibility with the rest of them. Tiny was never a bad kid, so I felt bad even though I had no choice but to do *something*. I remember getting almost emotional about this Tiny incident. I had to wipe him out in front of the other eleven guys. I couldn't allow him the kind of freedom on the floor I was giving him and not make him adhere to the rules and regulations the rest of the players were subject to.

Let's face it, Abe Lemons was thinking the right way when he explained why he didn't impose curfews on players. The reason, he said, was that you always catch your best player violating curfews. As a coach you hope you don't have to butt heads with the star. It can have disastrous results, maybe even cost you your job. With the Royals, even losing Tiny wouldn't have made that much difference. This wasn't Milwaukee with Kareem. We weren't going to make the playoffs with or without Tiny Archibald. There wasn't that much at stake, so I could be my own person.

We gave it, shall we say, the old college try in Cincinnati without great success. In Kansas City, however, we had Tiny to sell, and his name certainly came through for us. Joe Axelson knew the turf, and he worked 14 hours a day. He was a bright guy and knew what bases to touch. We let Tiny score his thirty-five points a game, hoping that would interest people, but by doing that we didn't get the right chemistry among the other guys to build a solid team for the future. Ultimately, I figured, "Where are we going? Why *not* go with the one-man concept?" What did we really have to lose? In the end, none of it mattered. The franchise is now located in Sacramento.

The NBA has expanded to Miami and Charlotte and is preparing to increase again by moving in to Orlando and Minneapolis. If anything, this league should consider shrinking down to 16 teams. Then I think we'd have a pretty good league.

Of course I'm old-fashioned and probably a bit naive. I'm interested in the quality of play and the integrity of the game. The owners are interested in the $32.5 million they are taking in from each of the new franchises. NBA Properties is drooling over the prospect of Florida, the fourth most populous state, finally joining the league. We're not on the same wavelength on the question of expansion, the NBA and me.

Everything is commercial now. There are stringent business guidelines laid down before new franchises come into the league. So many season-ticket commitments. So much parking. So much guaranteed radio and TV revenue. I hope they remember to buy uniforms. When the Chicago Packers came into the league in the 1940s, the only question was, "Can you get a gym?"

I should add that Commissioner David Stern and his colleagues have done an extremely effective job of marketing and promoting the NBA. In addition, they have handled the management–player relationship with the least amount of friction and with almost no threat of a strike. They have pioneered in developing fair and effective policies for addressing the drug problem and in opening up opportunities in coaching and management for blacks.

The pros are in it for the money. At least there's no hypocrisy, the way there is in the colleges. College people point their fingers at the pros and cluck about this and that. Meanwhile, you've got college presidents, athletic directors, and coaches all breaking rules and prostituting young players. Both the pros and the colleges are out to win and make money. The only difference is that the pros are up front about it.

But let's not kid ourselves. There is no artistic demand for expansion. I'm not at all sure the city of Miami is clamoring for a team, by the way. All I know is the product will now be diluted. Ticket prices will go up, anyway, and everyone will complain about the draft because the colleges are producing fewer good big NBA players.

The new teams may take years to become competitive. You don't need the last three or four players on an NBA team, and guess who will comprise the rosters of the new teams? Players from the bottom four spots on the roster of the current teams. Every time you expand, you increase the percentage of those who will not be competitive, for a longer period of time.

Dallas is said to have done a great job, but Dallas's success was due in large measure to the stupidity of Cleveland during the Ted Stepien regime. They had so many extra first draft picks acquired from Cleveland that they could afford to make mistakes such as Bill Garnett and still survive.

Good luck to the new teams. The NBA is a cold-blooded league. In general, the only way to help yourself is from the top. If you're at the bottom with an unknowledgeable owner, you're in trouble, especially if he is a meddler. Expansion teams must be very careful, because the piranha are swimming all around. They swoop in on the franchise and pick the bones, the way they did with Cleveland, which was, by that time (the early eighties), back to being an expansion team. The owner, Stepien, was impulsive and impatient, and finally the league had to step in and save him from himself.

The biggest hindrance these expansion teams will have is finding big men. There aren't enough to go around now. In truth, there never are. Even if we went to my dream sixteen-team league there wouldn't be enough quality big men to go around. And soon we'll be talking about twenty-seven teams. I see an increasingly hopeless scenario because the only way to win with a mediocre, or worse, big man is to surround him with very good talent. You might actually be able to go somewhere with Mike Gminski if you surround him with four good players. Willis Reed wasn't a truly great one in the mold of a Russell or a Kareem or a Wilt, in my opinion, but the Knicks surrounded him with great talent and won two championships. It seems to me it would be easier to create that situation with sixteen or eighteen teams than with twenty-seven.

I'm a radical anyhow. I've been an advocate of a smaller *basket* for years. That's right; I would reduce the circumference of the rim, making it more difficult to score. As the offensive skills improve, the league is going to have to deal with this question. I would do it now. Let's not waste any more time. It would be easier to do it now.

When the easiest part of the game is putting the ball in the basket, you might become bored with it. The league leaders are now shooting sixty percent from the floor. Artis Gilmore used to do it with dunks, but McHale now shoots 60 percent, and he's doing it with jump hooks and turnaround jumpers.

The college game is fun to watch. The players are energetic, and they go all out. The game is aided by the trappings of the cheerleaders and the enthusiastic fans. But the colleges had better be careful too. They're playing far too many games on TV now, and they're in danger of becoming too much like the professionals.

— 12 —

The Bird Years

I MUST CONFESS it didn't mean a whole lot to me when Arnold drafted Larry Bird in 1978. It didn't even mean much to me when he joined the team a year later. I had seen him briefly on TV, but I didn't think much about him, one way or the other.

I am a harsh critic. I judge players very stringently. I don't remember at what point I started to say that Bird was, in my opinion, the best player who's played the game up to now. I have a hunch it was before his second year.

Bird's talent was obvious, but his approach to the game is what caught my eye that first year. He accomplished a great deal that first year, making first team All-League and participating in the All-Star Game. We had all been brainwashed upon his arrival by reports that Bird didn't have excessive speed or wouldn't be able to rebound because he wasn't tough enough. Maybe there were some who wondered how much better Bird could get. That's a funny thing to say now, since Bird has improved so much since 1979. It's almost as if he's a different person.

By the end of Bird's first year, it was obvious the initial criticisms were pure rhetoric by his detractors. None of us knew how good Bird really was, including Arnold. He has admitted he had no idea Bird would reach the level he has. So not even Red knew. After watching Bird for a year I could see that while he didn't have the blazing speed he nevertheless had as much as needed for the situation. As far as the jumping is concerned, Bird demonstrated immediately he was going to be a top-flight rebounder.

The fact is that Bird has been able to accomplish in the NBA whatever he wants to. Given the pressures of the league and the sheer athletic ability of the people he competes against—they all have more speed, more rebounding ability, and in many cases more strength than he does—this is Bird's greatest feat. He has done well at whatever he needed to, and that includes three-point shots. For three years in succession, Bird has gone to the Three-Point Shot Competition at the All-Star Game, walked in and told the others they are battling for second place, and won. He just goes out and does it. I just hope Bird is smart enough to know when his physical skills start to diminish that it's time to cool it. I hope he doesn't put himself into a position where he can no longer perform.

Bird's first coach was Bill Fitch. Larry has always held him in high regard. Though Fitch was a drill sergeant, Bird had no difficulty adapting to his coaching style. Larry inherently respects authority and his work habits were well-established. There was little chance that Larry was going to displease Fitch and every chance that Larry would be held up as an example of how to go about your job for the others.

Bird didn't immediately take charge of the team. He believed there was a pecking order, and the man he placed at the top of the order was Dave Cowens. He wasn't looking to take the big shots right away. He thought that honor and privilege belonged to Cowens. And if Cowens wasn't in position to take the big shot, there was always Cedric Maxwell, then a devastating inside force. Bird had only one game-winning basket as a rookie.

Bird believed in Bill Fitch until the day Fitch left. When the Celtics lost their fourth straight game to Milwaukee in the 1983 playoffs—the team low in the Bird era—Larry stared into the cameras and said, "Fitch is the best coach in the league." The other players grumbled and were happy to see Fitch go. Bird defended him then and still does.

The fact is that Bird can play for any coach. It's the others who have a problem making the adjustment from personality to personality. When you're at Bird's level, coaching is almost incidental, at least on a personal basis. Jimmy Rodgers will start this season with the basic premise, "Bird's all set. Where do I go from here?"

Bird has continually advanced in all technical areas. He shoots better now than he did eight or nine years ago, and he has really made the three-pointer an art form. He has always rebounded well. He has averaged less than ten rebounds a game during the past couple of years as Kevin McHale picked up his own tempo and totals after becoming a starter in the 1985–86 season. Bird seems to increase his assists total each and every year. He makes clutch shots time and time again. And he is a very big deterrent on defense.

You hear a lot about Bird's defensive deficiencies. You won't be putting him on any point guards in the near future, I am sure, and the basic game plan of the Celtics is to put Bird on the weakest front-court offensive threat, whether he is a small forward, big forward, or center. It doesn't matter how tall the center is. Bird guards Tree Rollins and Randy Breuer, for example.

Bill Fitch always lived in fear of Bird being posted up, and the reason Fitch refused to play Bird and Scotty Wedman together when he had them was that he didn't want to worry about *two* guys getting posted up.

I've never had a great concern about Bird's defense. I'm not sure about the psychology of putting Bird on the big centers. I think I know what goes through Bird's mind when he's guarding Randy Breuer, who is 7'3". He picks his spots. He will give up the position inside to Breuer, and Breuer will get eighteen points, but if he played him tough from the beginning he would get four or six points. Breuer is not a bad shooter, but I have always felt Bird is somewhat indifferent to this post-up business until the last three or four minutes of the game. He is not easy to post up in the final minutes, when the game is on the line and he is fighting for position.

Bird can do whatever he makes his mind up to do, but as he gets older, he picks his spots more, especially when he is carrying the offense or doing heavy rebounding duty.

If I were coaching Bird, I wouldn't hesitate in any last minute situation to put him on *anyone*, whether it was a guard, a small forward, a big forward, or a center. He has the mobility and the smarts. I know that Bird would force something to happen. I know that the option the opposing coach had chosen would not work. Whichever guy he wanted to go to would be taken out of the play with Bird on him. That guy might pass to someone else and might win the game, but that's another story.

Beyond that last minute situation, there are valid reasons to reduce Bird's defensive responsibilities. As good as he is, or anyone is, there is only so much you can humanly accomplish night in and night out. You must focus his talents. Bird assumes he has to score thirty points a game *and* do his rebounding. Is it counterproductive to tack on the additional responsibility of a rugged defensive assignment? If he's got to worry about fighting through picks every time down the court, battling some monster for pivot position, or denying him up top, will it wear him out by the fourth quarter, or even get him in foul trouble? A coach has to be aware of this factor.

During the past several seasons, Bird seems to go through games or stretches of games in which he does things for his own amusement. In many home games, winning and losing is not really an issue. These games are in the "W" column before they start. Bird may do weird things or take some crazy shots to entertain both the crowd and himself. He is looking for ways to keep things interesting. But at no time does he lose sight of the basic precepts of the game.

Bird can afford to fool around because he really can control the flow of some games. There was a game last season in Chicago that made the point. Michael Jordan went crazy in the third period, but in the fourth quarter the show belonged to Bird. He scored sixteen tough points, and the Celtics won the game. At one point, Bird hit five great shots in a row. Chicago coach Doug Collins later said he couldn't believe how hard those shots were—and on a couple of occasions it almost seemed that Bird had waited extra long to take the shots. Bird explained that he *wanted* to be guarded so he could concentrate properly on the shots. "I wanted to draw the defense toward me," he said. That would make sense if his object were to draw defenders so he could pass, but in this case that wasn't his aim. Most players would rather not be double-teamed. It's hard enough with one player on you in this league. Bird's physical skills are not ordinarily diminished by the aggressive defensive measures that are taken against him.

Bird can seemingly adjust to anything. Against the defensive pressure of the NBA, he has an unparalleled shooting touch and God-given hand-eye coordination. He is crafty, smart, creative, committed, extremely competitive, intense, and in possession of a great instinct for the game. No player before this has put all these qualities together. Everyone else has weaknesses. Bird doesn't have any. When you talk about his weaknesses, you are simply talking about some areas that aren't as strong as others.

Bird's shooting range is totally destructive to the opposition. When a guy that's 6'9", almost 6'10", can hit a very deep two-pointer or a three-pointer, it adds an entirely new dimension to the problems of the defender. When you analyze any good player, you know that to defend a particular strength you must give up *something*. Bird goes to his right maybe seventy percent of the time, so obviously a defender might play him at least a little to the right. In doing so, he gives away the left. But Bird can go to his left, so he can burn the defender.

The next time, the defender decides to play Bird straightaway. Now, two areas are open for Bird to exploit. Percentages favor the defender if he allows Bird the twenty-two-footer, rather than letting him drive by him. But in Bird's mind the option of the long shot is always there without fear of extreme pressure. Again, it increases his advantage, having both the ability to hit the big shot and the willingness to take it. This increases his advantage over the hapless defender.

Auerbach would have loved to have coached Larry Bird. He would have loved Bird's basic toughness. Arnold always loved tough guys. I would classify Bird as a retaliator rather than an aggressor. When Bird's nose was broken last year by Blair Rasmussen, he didn't retaliate and try to break Rasmussen's nose. Rather, Bird tried to humble and embarrass Rasmussen with his talent.

Bird keeps coming back. That is the point. That's his toughness. He doesn't intimidate. Auerbach may say, "Why is he diving for a loose ball when we're up by twenty points with two minutes left?" But he secretly loves it. Arnold probably won't publicly say it because he doesn't want Bird to keep doing that unnecessarily. All these traits get Arnold's attention, however.

Then again, what probably gives Auerbach his greatest joy is the fact that he *chose* Larry Bird.

There are and have been a lot of great players, so why do I think Larry Bird is the best of them all? Start with his unselfishness. Then factor in his nightly effort. He is a throwback. The numbers are there, night in and night out. Every player believes he puts out all the time (with the conspicuous exception of ex-Celtic Cedric Maxwell, who once mused, "I wish I could play hard every night the way Larry does"), and likes to boast about it after the game. "I didn't play well, but, goddamn it, I gave 100 percent." Well, that is usually nonsense.

The fact is, Bird usually *does* give 100 percent. This is what every coach looks for in a player, but seldom finds in a talent package rivaling Bird's.

Obviously, I get turned on by Bird's passing game and his creativity more than his shooting and rebounding. He is the best passing forward who has ever played the game. He has the instincts and the skills to create opportunities and situations. He causes things to develop. Usually, you don't think of forwards as good passers. In Bird, however, you have a 6'9" forward who functions like a guard, both in mind and in skills.

And I am constantly amazed with Bird's shooting touch. I'll never forget seeing a couple of guys fall right

off the end of the Atlanta bench in amazement after a
shot Bird made against the Hawks the night he scored
sixty points in New Orleans. Most players, including
Kareem, go into a game with some apprehensiveness
about whether or not they will be able to get the shots
they want and if those shots will fall. I don't think Bird
worries about it.

Larry Bird goes into every game as if he was going
out on the playground to take shots with no defense.
When you get hot in a game of Horse, it's a terrific
feeling. Bird goes out there with two guys hanging on
him and makes the same shots—or tougher ones. And
he's got such versatility, so many weapons at his dis-
posal.

Bird loves the challenge. What makes the game fun
for him is to keep beating them down. The ultimate
tribute to Bird is that we can say he has gotten better
each of his nine years in the league. He has added
something new every year. Last year it was a new body.
No other great player in any sport has ever been able
to make that statement.

At no point during the first two decades of the Celtics'
prominence did anyone envision the arrival of a player
and personality who would encompass the "Celtic Mystique." Celtics fans probably figured it was quite enough
to have had a Cousy, a Sharman, a Heinsohn, a Cowens,
a Havlicek, and, most of all, a Russell. Then came Larry
Bird.

More than any of us—perhaps more than all of us
put together—Bird bears the burden of celebrity. He
lives in the eighties, when media focus is far heavier
than it ever was in my day. We played out our little
scenarios in obscurity half the time. The damnedest
things would be happening in Syracuse and Rochester

and Ft. Wayne, Ind., but to people in Los Angeles or Houston or Miami, each was like the proverbial tree falling in the forest. There was no ESPN Sportscenter bringing you the up-to-the-minute NBA happenings in those days.

In our day we had tremendous rivalries with teams such as Syracuse and Philadelphia. Referees were more inclined to adopt a "let 'em play" attitude because to call fouls was to subject themselves to massive abuse. The fans were hostile and the atmosphere was threatening. It wouldn't take much to get stimulated in a game. Sooner or later you'd get bumped by an opponent, and you'd get pissed off, and that's when the fights would break out. You could literally get wiped out or killed but nobody would hear about it for two days.

Bird's frame of reference is different. I think I can relate to what is going on inside his head. Let me try to take you into the world of Larry Bird—how he sees the world, and how he reacts to it. His anxieties, his idiosyncrasies, his character faults, his strengths, his needs, and his basic instincts. I have been there, and I believe I share certain character traits with Bird.

Bird is sometimes frustrated with his teammates. I used to go through this same lack of patience, I suppose, simply because everything came so easily to me. You've got this God-given talent, and early in your career you haven't developed the patience to realize that your teammates just can't perform as effectively or respond to certain situations the way you would. You don't understand yet. Later, you understand that they are trying as hard as they can, and you develop the necessary compassion for the guys who can't do what you can do.

This is important if you are a playmaker, which Bird happens to be, despite the fact that he is a forward. You start picking your spots, but you get impatient nonetheless. Your ego is such that you become annoyed if you make an exceptional pass to a guy, but he takes three steps before putting the ball in the hoop, neutralizing your beautiful pass.

Bird also believes so strongly in "the cause," that losing pains him. To this day, I hate to get on the bus after the team has had its nose rubbed in it and hear guys talking about innocuous things. I can't relate to that. And from what I see, neither can Bird. He is a throwback.

Bird has reflected on this publicly enough times, such as when he openly criticizes his teammates for their lack of effort—who will forget the time in the 1984 Finals when he said the Celtics had played "like sissies" after being bombed by the Lakers?—or for not wanting to win as badly as he does. I don't know that Bird's response to losing is something you ever get over because I suspect it is an inborn trait.

Bird thrives on the frequency of games. It's not like football, where you have to wait a week to get back out there and alter the situation. If the Celtics lose badly, Bird wishes there was a doubleheader so he can go right back at the other team.

I have never been able to observe him closely enough to know for certain just how excruciating losing is for Larry Bird, but the outward signs indicate that it bothers him a great deal. It's pretty obvious he hurts longer and deeper than the other players. This trait isn't related to his having more talent than they have—you would think, if anything, it would be the other way around. Auerbach would have loved coaching him for that reason. Those were the days before rock 'n' roll in the locker room. We used to sit in silence after a loss. There was no drinking, frolicking, or telling jokes. The atmosphere on the bus, plane, or train reflected what had just occurred. Sure, there are limits. I had an assistant coach named Jack Magee who later coached at Georgetown.

He said that if a kid asked him how bad he was supposed to feel after a loss he would say, "The same as you would if your mother or father died." He'd tell me that story with great glee. Whoa, Jack. That's ridiculous, and yet in my mind you should be inconsolable after a loss. It should hurt badly enough that you don't want it to be repeated.

That is how you stay on top and continue to be Larry Bird, best basketball player in the world. You have got to complement that approach with talent. That's how you sustain it. In any event, we thought we wouldn't see any others who felt this way. Bird is the exception. He seems to function this way.

When you're Larry Bird, you have a tremendous need for privacy. Off the court, you are insecure and sometimes frightened of the world. You have not yet gained the poise and sophistication to deal with the pressures of being thrust to the top, so you want to hide. You get better at dealing with it all, but you are never comfortable. You know you are not a rocket scientist, but more and more you must expose both your strengths and your weaknesses.

As time goes on, you must expose your weaknesses in more varied areas than your strengths. You are constantly experiencing emotional highs and lows, as you move from your moment on the floor, where you are the best basketball player in the world, to areas where you feel completely insecure. For the jock, there is absolutely no preparation as you move from one area in our society to another. Everything is done by the seat of your pants.

Look at the typical transition today. You go from playing ball in the schoolyard to somebody giving you a college scholarship, to the NBA, and then maybe to being a coach or an athletic director, or maybe even becoming a TV analyst. You have absolutely no training for any of the areas you are being thrown into.

In all these areas, you are being asked to function as well as you did as a jock. Whether it's getting up in front of an audience of 800 people—anything other than being on the playing floor, where you function with such confidence—you have to cope with a frightened feeling.

You can enjoy people in small groups but be terrified of being adrift in large gatherings without protection. You just don't enjoy people in large numbers. You yearn to be able to pick your nose in private, use the wrong fork, be sloppy or loud, or just be yourself, rather than being stared at. After a while, you become paranoid.

To this day, I can go into a place where not one person recognizes me and yet that is not the case in my mind. As a result, I am *never* comfortable. I can imagine Bird's feelings, especially at this point in his career. Even when I played, if one person came over it meant that every other person in the place was watching too. It means you can't eat a piece of chicken with your hands.

I have great empathy with Bird in this regard. When Bird is on the cover of *Sports Illustrated*, the problem is really magnified. He will tell you this. For the next week or two, he knows his life is really going to be chaotic. I used to go into hiding anyway, but even more so when I was on the cover of a magazine. You really feel trapped if you're in, for example, an airport.

It's funny how the ego manifests itself. When Auerbach first wrote a book, every time he had us in an airport he would run us over to the newsstand, point to it, and say, "That's my book. That's me." He would go out of his way. Of course, poor Arnold has changed. He has now gotten his due. He is a celebrity. He is a personality. His ego, I hope, has been satisfied. But in those days, nobody cared about the coach. Arnold wasn't getting anywhere near the recognition he deserved to receive. He had to call people's attention to himself to get the proper acknowledgement.

Bird's situation is just the reverse. He has to go deeper into his shell in walking through airports, and, every time he walks by a newsstand his picture is staring out from the cover of a magazine.

I won the MVP in 1957, which, theoretically, made me the best player in the game for that season. Bird is the best player ever. The problem is much greater for him. The comparison between my ghetto background and his small town country background is interesting. I am really most comfortable, even now, in my own bailiwick, where I can control the circumstances, so to speak. Bird appears to be most comfortable going back to French Lick, Ind., and hanging out with his old buddies. You enjoy being singled out as being the best in your business, but you inherently reject a lot of the fame that goes with the distinction. I stayed in my room. I had my meals sent up. I went to gyms to shoot at 6:00 in the morning, or did my pregame shooting at 5:00 P.M. Bird does the same. He shoots at 5:00 P.M., before the crowds come in.

Nobody on the team works harder than Bird. This is despite the fact that the game is easier for Bird. The mediocre player understands that he has to work hard, but nobody outworks Bird. The fact that Bird is the best player in the world and continues to put in the effort he does stems, I think, from a basic insecurity we all have. Once you reach the top, you want to stay there.

Some day Larry Bird is going to have a tremendous conflict. He'll be inclined to quit, and the Celtics will offer him a lot of money not to. His frugality will come out, despite the fact that he may have twenty, thirty, or forty million dollars put away. Bird's frugal instincts will tell him to accept a whopping offer to keep playing. Yet his pride in wanting to leave the game with his legacy intact, and being thought of as perhaps the best player to have come along at that point, will create a deep conflict within.

For the dollars we are talking about, I would probably have tried to stay in the NBA until I was 41, or until Russell went. But it won't be an easy decision for Bird. Havlicek didn't quit because he couldn't play anymore. He quit because he simply didn't enjoy coming to work every day. After he saw Bird, John said he wished he'd known someone like this was coming. He would have hung on for the opportunity to play with Bird. As it was, there was a one year gap between the two. We all have our standards. If the money were right, I wouldn't have minded having my individual station diminished a bit if the team had continued to be successful. I wouldn't have been hurt that badly.

Bird won't *need* the money. Soon, Robert Parish and Dennis Johnson will be gone. Brad Lohaus and Mark Acres may come along as players, but I assume that this team will continue to go downhill further and further. Perhaps the Celtics are entering a period of mediocrity. There will be no more Robert Parishes to pull out of the hat. The state of the team will influence Bird's decision to retire. The combination of insecurity and pride means you'd like to leave the game with the proper timing.

We are talking about image here. That was all-important to me because I wanted to use my fame to set up the rest of my life's work. My name was going to carry me through. We must assume Bird will retire with all the money he will ever need. But he still may not be able to relate to that money. His background prevents him from doing that. His frugality is inbred.

Frugality is a trait many jocks have. We are all products of our environments. I turn off lights when I leave a room. Occasionally I take the shampoo and soap home from the hotels. I am forced to go to banquets, and I hate every minute of it so I charge $5,000 each. Bird charges $40,000, and he doesn't accept invitations anyway.

In my opinion, the worst thing to be in this society is a half-assed celebrity. By that I mean being a celebrity who doesn't earn enough money to isolate him- or herself from the public. You literally become a prisoner in your own room or your own house. Show business people such as Sylvester Stallone can afford to hire bodyguards, but if you are either too frugal or don't earn enough, you can't afford such luxuries.

This is the position I was in twenty-five years ago. Making $30,000 a year doesn't allow you to build a wall to protect yourself. It's like being a show business star who's on the way out and no longer generating the old income. But because of past reputation, the star must still attempt to cloister him- or herself. You get out of the spotlight and all of a sudden it's over, but you still need protection from your fans. You either adapt or you hide. Bird can afford to hide. I would have done the same thing, if I could have.

Bird may be dealing with jealousies. When you're on top, you are not aware of your teammates' jealousies. I thought if I handled my role as captain and team leader properly, without taking advantage of my position, my teammates would admire me. I was hurt and surprised later when I discovered their true feelings about me. I have been through that one. It takes time and sophistication to understand the process.

For very practical reasons, teammates will always

say the "right thing" in public. You are The Man. They don't want to piss you off. You are into your ego trip, so you really believe that they are not feeling anything for you but great admiration. You are just a great player, and all that.

If Larry thought about it, he would see this phenomenon manifesting itself as long as six years ago. Remember when Harvey Catchings shattered his cheekbone in February of 1982? Bird was forced to miss five games. Well, the team went off to Texas and swept the Rockets, Mavericks, and Spurs without him, and they played with the enthusiasm of a high school team. Why? They wanted to show the world, and themselves, what they could accomplish *without* the great Larry Bird. Their pride came to the surface.

Bill Fitch was the coach, and his own ego came into play. He brought Bird back as a sixth man out of necessity. But when the team continued to win, he kept Bird coming off the bench as a sixth man far longer than was necessary. He enjoyed winning this new way. It made him a coaching genius of sorts.

After the years go by, you understand this better. I was hurt when the year after I retired the team dedicated the season to winning without me! "God," I thought, "these are my friends. What are they doing?" Now I understand perfectly what Arnold was doing. He had found the perfect motivating factor every coach seeks. I'm sure Heinsohn came in and said, "Let's win without Russell," but, of course, he didn't have the players to do so, so he probably didn't make it too public. If you're the coach, you use whatever weapons you can to motivate the team. As a player you eventually share these feelings. When it comes your turn to slide from the top or when you are in situations where you are not the top dog, you understand it more completely.

Initially, it is a jolt. It is traumatic. But it eventually helps you to mature.

Your experience just doesn't match up with everyone else's when you're Larry Bird. You're simple and straightforward in your relationships because of the supreme confidence you have in your special talents. If you get into coaching, you see the difference between the gifted ones and the rest. Even now, nine years after first seeing Larry Bird play, I am amazed at the miraculous, spectacular plays he improvises each night. I am fascinated by the moves he can manufacture so quickly, yet to Bird this is the easiest thing in the world. The guy with the mediocre talent has to work so much harder at it.

My behind-the-back passes used to have people asking all kinds of questions. I remember the first time I did it in college. I just did it, and everyone said, "God, you must have worked at *that*." But it was the first time I had done it. It happened to be what the play called for, so I did it. Thank God I had the talent. Bird does the same kinds of things, night after night. I am sure the casual observer can't believe it comes that easily.

The image of true greatness is earned by only the very few. You'd like to leave it intact in the minds of the people. You don't want to diminish it by staying one year too long. Bird will have that choice to make. I think this is also what causes him to work as hard as he does. When you have his talent you are aware that to some degree what you have accomplished is as dead as yesterday's newspaper. You must repeat your act every time you go out there. As the top player in the league, you literally can't afford a mediocre game.

Most great players don't significantly expand "their games" much beyond the way they play during the first three or four years. Bird is a very conspicuous exception. As a rule, a player of his caliber comes into each new season just making certain he can maintain his level of consistency. In my mind, this is all Larry Bird has to do. After a certain time in the league, I never worried about it. It's not like you're learning new moves. You want to maintain the sharpness of your game. How many shots do you have to take to accomplish this? How much of a difference does the shooting before a game really make? But in Larry Bird's mind, there is a base he must touch. Again, it is the fear and the pride. You are afraid that if you don't follow your particular routine and do this and do that, if you have a bad game you have screwed up.

So every year Larry Bird does what most great players don't do: he develops new moves. He adds something. One year it's a lefthanded shot. Another year it's one-on-one moves. In the summer of '87, it was a jump hook. I thought Bird fell in love with the shot a little too much last season, but he couldn't help himself. It was his new toy.

The summertime work is fun for Bird. It's a new summer challenge. All of us enjoy doing the things we do well. The fact that Bird knows he has the talent to develop whatever comes into his mind into new weapons makes it extremely enjoyable for him. How many other top jocks today function like this? The general approach is to take the path of least resistance. Bird said he developed the jump hook to use against Michael Cooper when posting up the Lakers' star defender. He never got to use his weapon because the Celtics didn't make it to the Finals against the Lakers. But how many other players would employ that thought process?

Michael Jordan, in my opinion, won't do this because he has such vast skill and jumping ability. The jumping gives him a feeling of excessive superiority, and he'll never feel the need to develop new moves. Bird knows he doesn't have the same physical tools as Jordan.

Dr. J was the forerunner of Jordan with the high

wire act, and he did make an adjustment, developing himself into a better outside shooter as his career went on. I think he had a basic shooting touch to begin with. He just never focused on the outside shot when he didn't need to. All of a sudden Erving had to complement his driving moves because opposing teams were closing down the lane. They were giving him the outside shot, and he adapted. Julius Erving never became a great shooter, but he was more than adequate.

Bird's adaptability will always serve him well. You can have *too* much raw talent if it handicaps your desire to learn the intricacies of the game. There will always come a day when your vertical leap will diminish by several inches, or your quickness will slow by a step, leaving you a step and a half behind people you used to blow by. But you can survive nicely if you've got a fundamental understanding of how the game should be played. Don Nelson never had any speed to speak of, even when he was young. But he was *always* open. Obviously, he knew something about how to play the game.

David Thompson and George McGinnis—especially poor George—are two excellent examples of players with raw talent. Thompson ruined himself with drugs, but McGinnis did himself in by being unable to adapt to Mother Nature. When things stopped going his way, George had no clue what was going on. His game deteriorated quickly. He lost all confidence at the foul line, and then stopped doing things that would get him there to avoid the embarrassment of bricking up a pair of free throws. McGinnis wound up like some sort of extinct species.

A true superstar creates a climate in which his teammates can overachieve. He takes the pressure off them by virtue of a single skill—Bill Russell's shotblocking, for example—or skills. It's not quite the same thing when Michael Jordan is averaging thirty-four points a game and the next guy is averaging twelve. The Bulls talk and talk about the need to broaden their scoring base. It will be interesting to see if they can do it despite the fact that Jordan's game is so individually styled. From time to time, Jordan will hit the free man after penetrating to the basket, but generally his first thought is to create opportunities for himself. His game doesn't lend itself to team play, the way Magic's and Bird's do.

The Bulls' Charles Oakley screamed and screamed about not getting the ball, and now he will have to do his screaming in New York. I don't know how much better Oakley will be able to score even if they do give him the ball, but now we'll find out. Bill Cartwright was brought into Chicago so they can throw him the ball, or so they say. Will Jordan really adapt to the presence of another legitimate scoring threat on the Bulls? We'll see if he can relate to that.

Leadership manifests itself in many ways. Bird is a throwback to the old days, when we all had to constantly prove our manhood by playing hurt. We see Bird doing it constantly: popping up after being cold-cocked, battling through colds, flu, and fever. It would have been an embarrassment for any of us to sit out with trivial ailments, and Bird is cut from that same bolt of cloth. This past season he bounced back immediately after breaking his nose and sustaining a serious eye injury. He came right back wearing goggles, which he hated for just about every reason. But he played with them, and he played very well. Keep in mind that the day Bird injured his eye, he scored thirteen points before the injury and eighteen afterward.

When Bird broke his cheekbone in '82, he finished the game. "Let me in there, coach," he said. He is always proving his manhood. If you're a star and you have that kind of motivation, it has more impact than you recognize. Whatever you do when you're on top has more impact. The guy down at the bottom of the bench can do all these things and nobody will notice. The blood can be pouring out of him and nobody will care. You have got to recognize that when you are at the top of the heap what you do creates much more drama. It generates much more of a response from the observer and creates a greater legend. We all love this sort of drama.

Everyone said Bird wouldn't play with the goggles, but when it came down to wearing them or not playing, he put the things on and played with his usual aggressiveness. He is always diving for loose balls, whether there are two minutes left in the game and he's up by twenty or the score is tied in the final ten seconds. It is the only way he can play. It's an urge to prove himself, over and over. It overshadows his good sense, but it is effective. This is the spirit that, when coupled with talent, wins battles, elections, corporate wars, and NBA championships. It creates legends. Stories become magnified over the years. It's also the kind of pride that may very well drive Bird from the game at the conclusion of his current contract (which expires at the end of the 1989–90 season), or, at least, a year or two earlier than his fans would want.

Bird has always been the way he is. I read in Frank Deford's interesting article in *Sports Illustrated* about Bird's reaction when he dislocated his right index finger playing softball. He yelled for someone to pull it back in so he could finish the game. That is the finger that was never properly treated and is a misshapened mess as a result. What a perfect illustration of Bird's spirit.

If that kind of competitive spirit is your bag, you

really don't have any control over it. You are going to respond in the way you do, even if eight qualified people tell you you're being foolish. You really can't help yourself. You are locked into that character trait. That is simply the way you are going to behave under those circumstances until they carry you out.

It is this attitude that enables Bird to take his ability and do something special with it. He has the killer instinct. The talent and psychological traits that have come together in Bird are seldom wedded. I am sure there are countless examples of people with talent in whatever field of endeavor who underachieve. They have great talent or great instinct, but they can't complete the package.

Russell didn't have Kareem's complete range of skills. But on the court he was a mean bastard; that's what made him so effective. Kareem doesn't have Russell's killer instinct. It all comes together in Bird. I don't believe there has ever been another player who has all of his mental and physical talents.

It seems odd to be talking about Larry Bird's impending retirement as he comes off as good a season as he's ever had. But he's the one who continually insists he is "95 percent sure" he will retire when his contract expires after the 1989–90 season.

Bird has not spelled out publicly why he is thinking about retiring when it's obvious he could perform well enough to be a major asset for many years to come. But I think I can jump inside his head and figure out some of the things going through his mind.

Larry loves to tease. He always says "95 percent." Once he upped that to "98 percent." He always leaves the door slightly ajar. He knows he is in a wonderful position. He does like money. He may not need any more than he's already got, but he likes the idea of making more. He kidded once last year, "Well, if some-one wants to pay me five million dollars, I'll listen."

It will be an interesting dilemma for the Celtics. Bird will be thirty-three years old when his contract runs out. He will be in good shape, barring an unforeseen physical setback. He's younger physically now than he was seven or eight years ago because of what he's learned about conditioning. The Celtics will have to give in and pay him an astronomical amount, whether they want to or not. Remember that the saving grace of Larry's game is that it doesn't depend on jumping or even running fast. He will make as good an adjustment to athletic old age as anyone ever did.

So what would drive him out? Suppose the Celtics become a .500 team. If that's the case, I wouldn't blame him for wanting to leave. If Robert Parish is gone or is suddenly nonexistent, Bird will be inclined to leave.

He will have twenty or thirty million dollars. It wasn't quite that way for those of us who came before. I returned for different motives. I was very careful. I knew I was going to leave with an untarnished image. I was playing well, but I wasn't at the top of my game. I was able to hide it with the strength there was behind me (Russell, in other words).

I wanted to protect my name because I knew I was going to have to exploit it for the next twenty or twenty-five years, which, thank God, I have, one way or the other.

Larry will want to protect his image, but not because he'll need it to earn a living. That's already been taken care of. We're in a new world. Larry's got his money salted away. He doesn't care about going to Europe or living in a two million dollar house. I find it hard to believe he will be able to wean himself from the game easily, however. Believe me, it is a frightening experience.

This speculation about Larry's retirement could soon

be moot. As this is written, his agent, Bob Woolf, is negotiating with the Celtics for an extension of Bird's contract. Woolf's goal is to make his client the highest-paid team athlete of all time. The Celtics' goal is an extension of Bird's contract.

Heavy is the burden of being the best in any field, of having to prove it every day in a competitive society. For the first time in your career you come to the realization that your physical skills have peaked and that maybe, just maybe, when you point to that centerfield wall you can no longer hit it out on demand. I went through this experience. It is traumatic and terrifying. Bird experienced it for the first time during last season's playoffs.

He had never before underachieved with everything on the line and when giving his complete mental and physical effort. In the 1988 playoffs his opponents were actually able to contain him on their terms rather than on his. In past years he had been stopped or at least somewhat neutralized on occasion by Michael Cooper, but then he'd always been able to go to his passing and playmaking options and create something for his teammates. This past year both Dominique Wilkins for Atlanta and Dennis Rodman for Detroit, with a lot of help from their friends, were successful in stopping Larry Bird from functioning on a basketball court for long periods of time the way he would have preferred. It had never happened before. Just as Larry tried to develop an anti-Cooper weapon (the jump hook) the previous summer, I'm sure he spent long hours this past summer searching for a possible solution, an anti–Wilkins/Rodman weapon.

There isn't any solution, of course. What happened to Bird in the playoffs happens to all the great ones. It's called getting old. In an individual sport (tennis or golf, for example) it is even more frightening because you are out there in your funny clothes and your giant reputation in front of millions on TV. All by your lonesome. Very scary and lonely. In a team sport, if you're fortunate to be surrounded by strength in the form of good, solid players, you can hide it much better and can neutralize it for much longer than if you are with a weak unit. The biggest problem you must deal with is yourself and your ego.

All the great ones become very macho and always want to be thought of as the "go to" guys at crunch time. Well, guess what? Your role now must occasionally, and then more and more, be as a decoy. You will continue to have the "go to" reputation based on the fear that you've created in your opponents over the years, but now you must create opportunities for your teammates rather than try to do it yourself.

The requisite for this option is having talented teammates, as I've said, and the creative and passing skills to implement this strategy. I was fortunate in having these God-given talents. Bird has them, too.

When it comes to crunch time, don't call your own number. Instead, do all you can to simulate the scenario the opponent has seen for years but with the intention of having someone else finish the play. Not every time. Don't become predictable. Do it enough to keep the "bad guys" off balance. Use the aging process to your advantage instead of letting it become a negative.

I did it for the last three or four years I played with Russell, Sam Jones, Heinsohn, and Havlicek his first year. Bird has the same kind of talent as in Parish, DJ, Ainge, McHale, and perhaps a few of the younger players. Fans won't notice the deterioration in Larry during the regular season games this year. Opposing teams simply don't come up with the sustained intensity and the ferocious defensive effort during the long season that they are able to summon for the playoffs. They pick their spots. This will allow Bird to be every bit as effective during the coming year as he was in the 1987–88 season. It's in the playoffs that, in my judgment, he must go to Plan B and play to his teammates. He's made all the necessary adjustments up to now. It will be interesting to see how he handles perhaps his most critical challenge.

From time to time, the idea of Bird finishing his career in, say, Indiana comes up. If I were counseling him, I would say, "Are you out of your damn mind?" I would never advise him to do that. I think he could damage his reputation. Those things don't work out. Johnny Unitas went to San Diego, Willie Mays to the Mets. Bad ideas.

As you age, the fans who have been watching you destroy opponents for so many years expect you to function at the old level. You come in, thirty-four or thirty-five years old, and you know you are not going to be the same player you once were. You can do yourself so much harm, and put yourself in such an uncomfortable position. I can see Bird hanging in with Boston and making a few million dollars more. But if I were him, I would never consider anything else, even in Indiana.

Bird's decision to play or not to play will come down to whether his feeling of personal satisfaction intersects favorably with the team situation in 1990. Let's assume Bird and the Celtics are finished moving upward. That is all he has ever known. Any other state of affairs has been a jolt. Bird has never started a season, with the possible exception of his first, in which he didn't honestly think his team was good enough to win the NBA championship.

Bird will know he isn't getting any better. He could compensate for this in his own mind by being more reckless. If it doesn't make sense for Bird to be diving for a loose ball when the Celtics are up by twenty points now, it will make even less sense in the future, which is why he might choose to do it. In other words, he may decide to show them why he's still number one. Don't *tell* them why, show them. That's as good as any way, in his mind. Do reckless things other players, especially other great players, aren't doing. That magnifies his position even more.

Bird is typical of great stars and show business people. When people come up to him and tell him he's the greatest, he is embarrassed. I used to hear that, and I wanted to run away. You don't know what to say in response. You blush, yet you want people to continue to say these things.

As long as you're playing you can deal with it. You put your positive traits in action, triggering these comments you say you don't want to hear in person.

If an ordinary player does the things Bird does, they go unnoticed. But when you are Larry Bird, those things have more impact. That's how legends grow. You are also not unaware that the stories become exaggerated as they are repeated. In a few years, Bird coming back from a broken nose will become Bird coming back from a broken leg with the bone sticking out of it. You're proud of this image, but you're not exactly sure how you're supposed to live with it.

I am confident Bird will make a mature and informed decision. Bird's shyness has always been misinterpreted by the public. If you rode the Celtics bus, you would never characterize Larry Bird as being shy. He needles everyone. People have misread his public shyness as snobbishness, but the truth is that it takes a long time to build confidence and be comfortable in large groups if that is not your basic personality. At the 1988 All-Star shindig in Chicago, comedian Jay Leno sat on a simulated "Tonight Show" set and interviewed some of the All-Stars, poking around for laughs. Magic and

Isiah did very well. But Bird and Michael Jordan got up there and bombed. It was a combination of shyness and being in a position where neither functions well.

Bird is fine in other public situations, however. His opinions remain simple and straightforward. He has developed enough confidence and sophistication to candidly state them. He does not play mind games. He shows what he feels and thinks. He doesn't have the politician's need to say what he is *supposed* to say. He is developing opinions in areas other than basketball —on drugs, for example—and stating them, which he wouldn't have done a few years ago. That's a positive step. Many in his position would remain silent.

Bird could quit right now with nothing left to prove. The team is still competitive, but in the not-too-distant future it will enter a different phase. Being on top for so long creates hostility and animosity on the part of the opposition and the fans. As the Celtics go down, that hostility will be focused on Bird. If he is the best player, so to speak, on the team, he has got to know this. It will be hard for him, because he loves to retaliate against opponents. If he no longer has the tools to do so, it will be traumatic. He might not be able to fight back adequately. Remember Paul Seymour and his life's ambition to shove the cigar down Auerbach's throat? I don't think Larry has antagonized anyone to that extent, but that kind of extreme hostility does develop, and it will all come crashing down on Bird's head if he's around during bad times.

Havlicek stuck around and took it, but with all due respect, John's situation was not comparable to Bird's. John will be remebered as one of the better forwards, maybe in the top five now. In a few more years, he may not even be in the top ten. He was an aggressive, hustling swing man anyone would love to have on his team. But when you're talking about Larry Bird, you're talking about the premier player of all time. He has so much more to lose than Havlicek. Bird has to be concerned about his pride and the frustrations of losing on a regular basis, although I must say it's difficult to envision any team with Bird on it being truly *bad*.

When Bird goes, the game will have lost its greatest practitioner. We're in an era with a Magic and a Jordan, and it's just my opinion, of course. But to me Bird encompasses what's good about basketball more than anyone. His talent takes pressure off teammates, allowing them to perform more effectively. They can key on what's important, rather than their statistics, when they play with Bird.

He passes, which helps everyone. He's involved in the rebounding. Most of all, he understands the personal dynamics of a basketball team. If you are a jackass, if you are selfish, if you are undependable off the court, you will ruin the effectiveness of what you do on the court. Bird is none of these things. His personality off the court enables him to interact successfully on the court. He makes the other players better.

Let's just hope that when he goes he doesn't take the Celtic Mystique with him. We have all been very, very spoiled.

— 13 —

The Celtic Mystique Today

THERE IS NO question that the advent of the satellite dish has greatly expanded the visibility of every other team in the NBA. But no team has benefitted from this exposure as much as the Boston Celtics.

I base this not only on what I see but also on what I hear. I have never covered another team on an ongoing basis as a broadcaster. It is certainly conceivable that the Lakers have a tremendous following, or that in the Dr. J era, the 76ers were immensely popular. I suspect the Chicago Bulls with Michael Jordan as the cornerstone are gaining in popularity. But in comparing notes with people who spend their time with other teams, I can safely conclude that the national interest in the Celtics dwarfs that of any other NBA team—even the five-time world champion Los Angeles Lakers.

When I first started broadcasting Celtics games for WBZ in Boston, we would get notes from people on the road asking us to say hello to so-and-so back in Boston. But once the satellite dishes began to proliferate, the game changed.

Now our arrival in every city is greeted by fans we have nicknamed "The Green People." They meet us at airports, in hotel lobbies, and in arenas wearing some sort of green and white Celtics paraphernalia. The autograph requests have increased ten-fold—maybe even a hundred-fold—and not just from NBA fans. These are *Celtics* fans. They are young. They are old. They may have followed the Celtics from afar for thirty years. They may be the sons and daughters of people who have followed the team for thirty years. In any case, they watch the games if they can, they listen if they can, and they subscribe to *Celtics Pride Magazine* if they're aware of it.

This is the manifestation of the Celtic Mystique. Something has been going on for over thirty years, and these people are deeply affected by it. I know of one fellow in Wisconsin, a school teacher no less, who was so distraught upon hearing that Larry Bird had injured his Achilles' tendon in Cleveland in November of 1987 that he called in sick. That's devotion.

The problem for me is that I am now in my old grouchy stage. For me, it is a pain in the ass. Sometimes I can deal with it better than at other times. The players never get a respite. You can't believe what goes on. You get on a bus at 1:00 in the morning, and they are there. They have sources of information like the CIA. We come back to the hotel late at night and people are waiting for us. I screamed at a couple once. Then I felt ashamed for having done it. The attention the Celtics get is overwhelming. Fans really take time to search out your schedule. They will sit in the lobby and wait all afternoon for the bus to depart. Once, we arrived in Philadelphia late and there was a little grey-haired old lady waiting for us.

The Green People are all over, and they drive some of the other executives in the NBA crazy. Stan Kasten in Atlanta kids us a lot about it. Jerry Colangelo in Phoenix just can't cope with the number of people in the arena wearing green shirts and hats when the Celtics come to town. They're big in Washington and Oakland, two cosmopolitan areas with a lot of transients. There are even a few resourceful people among the nightly 12,666 in the Portland Memorial Coliseum, where there hasn't been an official empty seat in about ten years. I also see a great number of Celtics jackets in the non-league cities as I travel around.

I am aware that vast numbers of people hate the Celtics as fervently as The Green People love them. The Celtics are the great polarizers of the NBA. Very few people who are interested in the NBA are neutral about the Celtics. But I'd venture to say that the ratio of Celtics lovers to Celtics haters is much in favor of the former.

There is probably no other team in the league that can make the following statement: No basket of ours ever goes uncheered.

The Lakers have won their cherished back-to-back titles, but I think we've seen the last sports dynasty in any real sense. No team will dominate the NBA for long periods again. The jock will struggle hard to reach the top of the hill. He just won't put out the effort necessary to stay on top.

You need a certain amount of luck to win at any time. We had it, and the Lakers had their share last season, too. Michael Cooper shot about thirty percent in the playoffs, but one night he beat Utah with his only basket of the game.

But most of all you need hard work to augment talent. For a year and a half I have watched the Celtics' motivation neutralized on the boards and on defense, the hard-work areas. They have been last in the NBA in steals and last in percentage of offensive rebounds for two seasons. That has to tell you something. They have control over these things. This was reflected in road losses, when they refused to get in the trenches and tighten their belts. They wound up losing two fifth games at home during the playoffs, and two games at home in one series to the Pistons, who beat them in six games. Detroit made a massive commitment to defense, and they got it from nine men. Let's see what happens "the year after."

Injuries play a role and other excuses play a role, but the overriding reason working against long-term team greatness and unity are guaranteed contracts. It is just the nature of the beast. When we are motivated and we are underdogs, we will overwork and over-achieve to reach the top of the mountain. Once we reach the mountaintop, and get our hands on all the goodies we find there, we fall off the mountain.

I have heard Auerbach say it and others say it, but not many want to say it out loud. They fear it will reflect on the integrity of the game. They say the players aren't trying as hard as they can often enough during the regular season. Players never admit that. The closest thing they say is, "I screwed up tonight, but I gave my all." I don't believe it.

The true impact of the Celtic Mystique is that people are attempting to imitate, or perhaps even improve on, the things Red Auerbach was preaching from the day I met him, thirty-eight years ago.

One of the essential dilemmas of professional basketball is this: How do you tell a guy who has been All-American, All-World, All-Sandbox, and everything else that now his skills lie in limited areas? Just concentrate on your passing and defense and forget your shooting.

Or else, concentrate on your shooting and forget about ever making the All-Defensive Team. Or, you can help us for ten or twelve minutes a game, but that's about it.

Who wants to hear that? Somehow, Auerbach always knew how to get this across. Good coaches today must do the same thing.

One of Arnold's great hallmarks was continuity, and I must admit that's harder to achieve today. Of all the amazing things about Auerbach, perhaps the single most fascinating thing he did was go nine years without a body-for-body trade. From the time he traded Mel Counts for Bailey Howell prior to the 1966–67 season until he traded Paul Westphal for Charlie Scott a few weeks following the conclusion of the 1974–75 season, the Celtics never made a player-for-player trade. Arnold picked up players on waivers. He bought player contracts. But he never made a single body-for-body exchange for nine full years on the calendar. He created a feeling of family, but he always let people know they were on trial. He knew how to keep the fires burning without allowing someone to think he was going to be roasted.

More than any team in the league, the Celtics have linked a player's name with that of the team. Think of all those great players who only performed for Boston. Russell, Sam Jones, K.C. Jones, Heinsohn, Ramsey, Sanders, and Havlicek played only for Boston. Throw away the seven games I played for Cincinnati in 1969, and you can include me, too. Sharman actually started out with the Washington Capitols but didn't play for them very long. From today's crop you can include the names of Bird and McHale, not to mention Ainge. And you know neither Robert Parish nor Dennis Johnson will ever play for another team.

This is a direct result of Auerbach's influence. With precious few exceptions, owners have allowed Auerbach to run the basketball team since 1950. Walter Brown certainly wasn't going to interfere very much. A lifelong hockey man, all he really knew about the intricacies of basketball was that good big men were preferable to good small men. That's why he didn't have to be sold on the virtues of drafting Charley Share over Bob Cousy. For thirty-eight years, the essential duties of a Celtics owner have been to kiss Red's ring, sign the checks, and be ready to accept the championship trophy.

There was one conspicuous exception: John Y. Brown, who created more mischief in one season than all the other owners—and since Walter Brown died there have been many—put together. John Y. had started in basketball with the Kentucky Colonels of the ABA, and he fancied himself a basketball wizard.

One day he explained why. "I've been in basketball for seven years," he explained. "If I had gone to medical school for seven years, I could be a brain surgeon."

Mr. Brain Surgeon was the one who took the three first-round draft choices Arnold had painstakingly acquired during the 1978–79 season and traded them to New York for Bob McAdoo, who was not a classic Celtic. He was a menace from the start, as Auerbach found out early that season.

The Celtics had been blown out at home, and following the game the brain trust retired to the team offices to mull things over. Arnold has always used his office as a sanctuary. It looks like a basketball shrine, and when Arnold is seated at his desk receiving visitors, he is like a potentate. He is never more at home than when he is playing the grand host in his office.

John Y. beat Red upstairs to the office. When Red arrived, John Y. piped up. "Well, well, well," he said. "Here comes our great leader now. Say something intelligent, great leader."

I was aghast. I was ready to come to the aid of my

old coach with my fists, as corny as that sounds. I whispered to John Y.'s partner, Harry Mangurian (who, fortunately, would buy out his partner at the conclusion of that dreadful season), "I'm going to have to punch that guy out."

But Red didn't acknowledge Brown. He let it pass. It was such a pathetic scene.

Red, of course, is still receiving visitors in his office. Mr. Brown is long gone. He was elected governor of Kentucky, and I hope he did a better job there than he did with the Celtics.

There is nothing romantic about what Auerbach has accomplished. He took advantage of every situation when he coached, and he has continually twisted or bent the rules as a general manager. But he has remained a step ahead of the competition for thirty-eight years. Who, for example, maneuvered to secure Bill Russell, without whom the Celtic Mystique could never have been born? Red Auerbach. Who saw the value of Dave Cowens? Bob Cousy did, but Red Auerbach was able to beat him to it. Who drafted Charlie Scott in the seventh round of the 1970 draft, even though Scott had already signed with the ABA? Red Auerbach. Who was able to trade the rights to Charlie Scott to Phoenix in exchange for Paul Silas when Scott jumped to the NBA? Red Auerbach. Who picked up the extra draft choice that allowed him to take Larry Bird a year early and set up the latest phase of the dynasty? Red Auerbach. Who traded for Kevin McHale and Robert Parish? Red Auerbach. Who drafted Danny Ainge after the kid had assured *everybody* who asked that he would play baseball for the Toronto Blue Jays? Red Auerbach.

Arnold can be cheap and unreasonable. When I went to him with an offer for $100,000 and change to coach the Royals in hand, he said, "Hang around for a year, and I'll start you at thirty grand a year." No sentiment there. He was just being expedient.

Arnold deserves all the credit for his hard work, knowledge, general expertise, and, yes, luck. But let's not overly romanticize things. Very often with the Celtics, as with everyone else, the credo was, "What have you done for me lately?" But it's hard to knock a man who didn't trade anybody for nine years.

With the exception of John Y. Brown, the owners all seemed to pay the proper homage to Red. They might all have big egos, but they were all smart enough to recognize that Red was the key to maintaining the Celtics' aura. Even then, the owners were essentially cold-blooded. They often lived 500 miles away, and the Celtics were often just a subsidiary, a branch office, to them. With that kind of ownership mentality—about as far removed from the emotional day-to-day approach of Walter Brown as you can get—the franchise can get into serious trouble.

John Y. Brown was the worst. The team was his toy, and he wanted to play with it. He didn't care about the Celtic Mystique, or anything else. Doing something spectacular like trading franchises was more important to him than anything else. That's how he wound up in Boston to begin with. He traded the Buffalo franchise to Irv Levin, who moved it to San Diego.

Given the fact that following the death of Walter Brown, the Celtics have been a corporate pawn, the Celtics could very easily have gone straight down the tubes after Russell's retirement had it not been for the presence of Auerbach. Arnold got so fed up with John Y. Brown's shenanigans in 1979 that he came very close to quitting and assuming a comparable post with the Knicks. Can you imagine that?

It is difficult to imagine the Celtics without Auerbach, and perhaps that has a lot to do with the amazing popularity of the Celtics, both nationwide and on an international basis. Bostonians who go abroad are continually astonished to encounter people wearing Celtics hats, T-shirts, jerseys, and shorts. The Celtics represent stability.

Clearly, something is going on. Performance is at the heart of it, of course. There would be no Celtic Mystique if the team had missed the playoffs ten straight years. Winning breeds camaraderie more than losing does. The Nets might be close by, but no one cares one way or the other. Nobody cares, because they don't win.

But the Celtics have been able to keep momentum through the sixties, seventies, and now the eighties. They have bounced back twice, the first time after Russell and Sam Jones retired together in 1969, and the second time after the John Y. Brown fiasco of 1978–79. Thank God Bird came along. Chance played a role in this, far more than anyone involved would care to admit. Auerbach had a lot to do with it, too.

For me, it all comes down to this: I am a Celtic. Even when I coached the Royals/Kings, I related completely to the Celtics. People have asked me how it felt to coach against the Boston Celtics, especially in the Boston Garden, where I have so many wonderful memories. I can tell you it was very difficult. Very difficult. It would have been extremely hard for me if we had been a competitive team. That would really have tested me. I mean, *really* tested me. On the other hand, it certainly made me more emotional trying to beat the Celtics.

I vividly remember my first game as a coach. It was in the Boston Garden. It was *very* traumatic. I really got weepy on that one. We pulled out a close game. It was so meaningful to come back and win that first game, even if we didn't win another game the rest of the year. Generally speaking, however, I really didn't have to cope with that much. It would have set off a deep conflict of interest if I had been a Laker coach and had to go against the Celtics in the playoffs. But that's different.

The experience of being a Celtic gave us all an identity we will carry as long as we live. When I broadcast, it is always "we." I fight this all the time. I get criticized for it all the time. It is so ingrained that sometimes I don't even know I am saying it.

I am thinking, "*We* need a basket." "*We* have got to get going." "*We* have to do this."

I can't jump up and down or anything, but I feel things. I watch Arnold across the way, and it's as if nothing has really changed. He's still a competitor. The referee makes a bad call and Red leaps to his feet. Partially it's because he is on the line. Partially it's for show. Generally, it's an offshoot of the old theory at work when he would try to get himself thrown out of the game to excite and stimulate the players.

Sometimes I want to scream. I actually find myself choking up at something that occurs out there on the court. This indicates a relationship that just can't be broken. It's there, and it will always be there. I will always relate to the Celtics, no matter which players' faces come and go or how I feel about them. I share something with them.

There *is* something that binds us old guys with Bird, McHale, DJ, Parish, and Ainge. It's something that makes us feel special, that makes us feel very proud to have been a part of the most successful franchise in sports history. As pissed off as I can sometimes get about Arnold, if something happened to him I'm sure I would break down and cry.

Thank God we were successful. Our memories are all warm. For us, being a product of our times has a lot to do with it. We had a closeness if only because we didn't have all the other distractions. We didn't have the financial opportunities players have today.

The only time Frank Ramsey calls me is when he's had a few. If my phone rings at 11:00 at night, I know it's Rams. He wants to talk about old times. He'll get weepy on the phone. He is sitting on his porch down there in Madisonville, Ky., just reliving the old days and saying how much fun it was. I only hope today's millionaire Celtic players are blessed with the "wealth" of those memories in their retirement.

THRILLERS BY WILLIAM W. JOHNSTONE

THE DEVIL'S CAT (2091, $3.95)

The town was alive with all kinds of cats. Black, white, fat, scrawny. They lived in the streets, in backyards, in the swamps of Becancour. Sam, Nydia, and Little Sam had never seen so many cats. The cats' eyes were glowing slits as they watched the newcomers. The town was ripe with evil. It seemed to waft in from the swamps with the hot, fetid breeze and breed in the minds of Becancour's citizens. Soon Sam, Nydia, and Little Sam would battle the forces of darkness. Standing alone against the ultimate predator—The Devil's Cat.

THE DEVIL'S HEART (2110, $3.95)

Now it was summer again in Whitfield. The town was peaceful, quiet, and unprepared for the atrocities to come. Eternal life, everlasting youth, an orgy that would span time—that was what the Lord of Darkness was promising the coven members in return for their pledge of love. The few who had fought against his hideous powers before, believed it could never happen again. Then the hot wind began to blow—as black as evil as The Devil's Heart.

THE DEVIL'S TOUCH (2111, $3.95)

Once the carnage begins, there's no time for anything but terror. Hollow-eyed, hungry corpses rise from unearthly tombs to gorge themselves on living flesh and spawn a new generation of restless Undead. The demons of Hell cavort with Satan's unholy disciples in blood-soaked rituals and fevered orgies. The Balons have faced the red, glowing eyes of the Master before, and they know what must be done. But there can be no salvation for those marked by The Devil's Touch.

Available wherever paperbacks are sold, or order direct from the Publisher. Send cover price plus 50¢ per copy for mailing and handling to Zebra Books, Dept. 3007, 475 Park Avenue South, New York, N.Y. 10016. Residents of New York, New Jersey and Pennsylvania must include sales tax. DO NOT SEND CASH.

J.J. MARRIC MYSTERIES

Time passes quickly . . . As *DAY* blends with *NIGHT* and *WEEK* flies into *MONTH*, Gideon must fit together the pieces of death and destruction before time runs out!

GIDEON'S DAY   (2721, $3.95)
The mysterious death of a young police detective is only the beginning of a bizarre series of events which end in the fatal knifing of a seven-year-old girl. But for Commander George Gideon of New Scotland Yard, it is all in a day's work!

GIDEON'S MONTH   (2766, $3.95)
A smudged page on his calendar, Gideon's month is blackened by brazen and bizarre offenses ranging from mischief to murder. Gideon must put a halt to the sinister events which involve the corruption of children and a homicidal housekeeper, before the city drowns in blood!

GIDEON'S NIGHT   (2734, $3.50)
When an unusually virulent pair of psychopaths leaves behind a trail of pain, grief, and blood, Gideon once again is on the move. This time the terror all at once comes to a head and he must stop the deadly duel that is victimizing young women and children — in only one night!

GIDEON'S WEEK   (2722, $3.95)
When battered wife Ruby Benson set up her killer husband for capture by the cops, she never considered the possibility of his escape. Now Commander George Gideon of Scotland Yard must save Ruby from the vengeance of her sadistic spouse . . . or die trying!